A Guide
to Consent

■

Edited by

Robert D. Dinerstein, JD
American University
Washington College of Law

Stanley S. Herr, JD, DPhil
University of Maryland
School of Law

Joan L. O'Sullivan, JD
University of Maryland
School of Law

American Association on Mental Retardation

Published by
American Association on Mental Retardation
444 North Capitol Street, NW, Suite 846
Washington, DC 20001-1512

The points of view expressed herein are those of the authors and do not necessarily represent the official policy or opinion of the American Association on Mental Retardation. Publication does not imply endorsement by the editors, the Association, or its individual members.

Printed in the United States of America.

Library of Congress Cataloging-in-Publication Data

A guide to consent/edited by Robert D. Dinerstein, Stanley S.
    Herr, Joan L. O'Sullivan
            p.   cm.
        Includes bibliographical references.
        ISBN 0-940898-58-6
            1. Informed consent (Medical law)—United States.
    2. Insanity—Jurisprudence—United States.
    I. Dinerstein, Robert D.   II. Herr, Stanley S.   III. O'Sullivan,
    Joan L.   IV. American Association on Mental Retardation.
    KF3827.I5G85   1998
    344.73'0412—dc21   98-47537
                                                CIP

TABLE OF CONTENTS

TABLE OF CONTENTS

TABLE OF CONTENTS

AAMR AD HOC COMMITTEE ON CONSENT

PREFACE

The American Association on Mental Retardation's (AAMR) *Guide to Consent* is an entirely new approach to issues of consent and choice by persons with mental retardation. It explores the policy, legal, and programmatic implications of topics vital to self-determination. It draws on concepts first explicated by this association in its *Consent Handbook,* published in 1977. That handbook grew out of the work of a subcommittee of the organization's Legislative and Social Issues Committee (1975–1976) and was edited by H. Rutherford Turnbull, III, Douglas Biklen, and James Ellis.

The *Guide to Consent* is the product of an ad hoc committee currently chaired by Cathy Ficker Terrill, vice president, AAMR. Committee members Stanley S. Herr, Joan L. O'Sullivan, and Robert D. Dinerstein edited the volume. Committee members who wrote chapters include:

- **Chapter 1, Introduction: Robert D. Dinerstein.** Professor Dinerstein is professor of law and associate dean for academic affairs at American University's Washington College of Law. He is former president of AAMR's Legal Process and Advocacy Division and a member of the President's Committee on Mental Retardation.

- **Chapter 2, Adult Guardianship and Alternatives: Joan L. O'Sullivan.** Professor O'Sullivan is a visiting assistant professor of law in the University of Maryland School of Law's Clinical Program and the author of *The Guardianship Handbook,* a guide to adult guardianship and guardianship alternatives in Maryland.

- **Chapter 3, Informed Consent for Health Care: Anne Des Noyers Hurley and Joan L. O'Sullivan.** Dr. Hurley is associate clinical professor of psychiatry at Tufts University School of Medicine and Tufts-New England Medical Center and director of clinical services at Bay Cove Human Services, Inc.

- **Chapter 4, Consent to Sexual Activity: Paul F. Stavis and Leslie W. Walker-Hirsch.** Mr. Stavis is counsel to the New York State Commission on Quality of Care for the Mentally Disabled. He has published extensively on the balance between sexual expression and protection from harm for people with mental retardation and developmental disabilities. Ms. Walker-Hirsch is a sexuality consultant, educator and private practitioner and co-creator of the CIRCLES series.

- **Chapter 5, Consent to Residential Options: Pam Lindsey.** Pam Lindsey, Ph.D., is an assistant professor of special education at Tarleton State University. She has published several studies concerning the consenting ability of adults with developmental disabilities and is the author of the consent policy statement accepted by CEC-MRDD in 1997.

- **Chapter 6, Capacity for and Consent to Legal Representation: Stanley S. Herr.** Professor Herr is president of AAMR (1998–99) and has held many positions within the organization. He teaches at the University of Maryland School of Law and is a Schell Senior Research Fellow of the Yale Law School.

- **Chapter 7, Capacity in the Courts: Robert D. Dinerstein and Michelle Buescher.** Ms. Buescher is a 1998 graduate of American University's Washington College of Law.

- **Chapter 8, Consent to Extraordinary Interventions: Robert D. Dinerstein, Stanley S. Herr, and Joan L. O'Sullivan.**

- **Chapter 9, Conclusion: Stanley S. Herr and Joan L. O'Sullivan.**

In addition, thanks also are due to Michael Glasser, visiting law student, and Colleen Hogan, Class of 1998, University of Maryland School of Law, and Pamela Gully, Class of 1998, American University, Washington College of Law, for their editorial and research assistance and to the leadership and staff of AAMR for their support throughout this project.

The membership of the ad hoc committee was designed to reflect a broad range of views and perspectives within the mental retardation field. In addition to the individuals listed above, the members included John M. Agosta of the Human Services Research Institute, Peter D. Blanck, professor of the University of Iowa College of Law; Jeffrey J. Fahs, M.D.; Leo Plotkin of the Florida Arc; H. Rutherford Turnbull, III, professor, University of

Kansas Beach Center on Families and Disabilities; and Nancy Ward of People First. Daniel Rosen, president and CEO of ARI, Inc., also served on the committee for a time.

The new *Guide to Consent* takes the overarching consent framework as largely given (chap. 1) and then examines in greater depth a wide range of areas: adult guardianship (chap. 2), informed consent/medical care (chap. 3), consent to sexual activity (chap. 4), program placement and home ownership (chap. 5), capacity for and access to legal representation (chap. 6), capacity and the courts (chap. 7), and miscellaneous areas in which the person's liberty and autonomy interests are especially strong (experimentation, aversives, sterilization, parental rights, and admissions to facilities and programs) (chap. 8). We then offer a brief conclusion with observations on some consent issues for the future (chap. 9).

These are not the only areas in which issues of consent are important, of course, but they do represent a fair sampling of some of the most critical life events for people with mental retardation. The change in format from the 1977 Consent Handbook reflects the realities of 20 years' further developments in law and policy, as well as the ad hoc committee's perceptions about which aspects of consent people in the field of mental retardation will find most helpful. It is also responsive to reports from the field that practical applications of consent law and practical examples in which consent issues arise are most useful.

This book records a project that is in continuous progress. New topics will constantly emerge. New cases, laws, and philosophies of habilitation will reshape the underlying terrain. No brief guide will eliminate the need for consultation on the specifics of the laws, regulations, and public policies of the reader's particular state. The editors, however, do believe that the *Guide to Consent* can be a starting place for ready answers, regional and local training sessions, and further research and debate. We also are certain that the next edition of this volume will be needed early in the next millennium.

It is our hope that this book will provide the framework for the continued and dynamic consideration of the role of consent in the lives of people with mental retardation and the lay and professional people with whom they interact.

Robert D. Dinerstein   *Stanley S. Herr*   *Joan L. O'Sullivan*

CHAPTER 1

Introduction

■

Robert D. Dinerstein
American University
Washington College of Law

N ow more than ever before, persons with disabilities are asserting their right to make major and minor decisions.[1] In making these choices, they have left behind institutional living and have entered the mainstream of life in the United States. They rely less on government-delivered services and more on natural supports. They attend school in inclusive settings. They work in conventional workplaces. Many live in the community in small homes or apartments that they themselves own or lease. They participate with friends in community recreational activities. They seek opportunities for sexual expression and to have and rear children. They increasingly advocate for themselves or seek assistance from lawyers and other professionals.

These changes have not relieved those who love and support those with mental retardation and other developmental disabilities from being concerned about issues of consent and choice. To the contrary, greater freedom and choice have created new situations in which the person's consent must be sought.

This revision of the 1977 *Consent Handbook* takes into consideration these and other significant changes in the world of developmental disabilities (e.g., Sundram, et al., 1994; Ellis, 1992). The following principles concerning consent will be found throughout this *Guide to Consent:*

---

[1] Throughout the *Guide to Consent, person* will be used to mean the person with mental retardation or other developmental disability. *Individual* will be used to mean someone other than a person with mental retardation or other developmental disability.

- American society places a strong emphasis on personal autonomy and a person's right to self-governance (Dinerstein, 1990, pp. 512–513). Society and law require people to give consent, or at least assent, to major decisions concerning the person's interests and values.

- All citizens are presumed to be competent or to have capacity to make decisions regarding their lives. A person with disabilities is presumed to have an interest in autonomy that is every bit as strong as the interests of those without disabilities. Put in constitutional terms, "people with mental retardation have substantial liberty interests that merit full protection" (Ellis, 1992, p. 1804).

- The ability to give consent presupposes the existence of three elements in the decision maker: *capacity, information,* and *voluntariness* (Ellis, 1992, p. 1796; Turnbull, 1977, pp. 6–13).

- As the importance of the interest increases, the need for more formal determinations of capacity to consent increases as well. For example, if the proposed action or decision would expose the person to significant physical or psychological risk, there should be greater assurance that the person's consent is valid (Turnbull, 1977, p. 1).

- Persons with mental retardation will not always have the cognitive, communicative, or educational capacity to make autonomous decisions, nor to give valid consent (Ellis, 1992, pp. 1782–1788). In such cases, the persons with mental retardation may need assistance in making decisions or expressing their consent.

- Assistance in decision making should offer the least restrictive intervention, and be for the shortest possible time, to maintain the principles of autonomy and self-governance. The assistance of lay advocates or family members is preferred to court-ordered determinations of incompetency or incapacity. Where court intervention is necessary, it should be as limited as possible (i.e., limited guardianship should be sought instead of plenary guardianship).

- Any assisting decision maker should consult with and solicit the views of the person with mental retardation.

- Assisting decision makers should use substituted judgment rather than a best-interests standard. That is, the decision should be based on what the person would have decided if the person were competent, rather than on what the decision maker believes would be best for the person (e.g., Superintendent of Belchertown State School v. Saikewicz, 1977). The substituted judgment standard requires the decision maker to know the person and his or her specific situation before deciding. This standard may require consultation not only with the person, but also with friends, self-advocates, family members, educators, and psychologists with whom the person has come in contact. When it is impossible to learn the person's desires, the decision maker must use his or her judgment about what is best.

- No one can make appropriate decisions without adequate information. Persons with mental retardation may need more information than others about a specific decision or background facts. Those seeking to obtain the consent of the person with mental retardation must seek out ways to enhance the person's knowledge base, and they must take extra care to communicate effectively. Those seeking consent must not confuse the person's informational poverty with his or her decisional capacity.

- For consent to be valid, it must be voluntary and uncoerced. We may think of coercion as extreme physical or psychological pressure, but it also exists in more subtle forms, especially for persons who have lived in institutions or other settings in which they had insufficient opportunities to give consent or make choices (Ellis, 1992, pp. 1786–1787). Those seeking consent are obligated to make sure that the person's consent is given freely and under noncoercive circumstances. This obligation is particularly difficult when the consent seeker directs a program or otherwise exercises power over the person with mental retardation.

- Which individual should request consent from the person? Careful thought should be given to this question and to the person's ability to make an independent decision or to refuse a request from that individual.

- The quest for autonomy must be balanced by the need to protect persons with mental retardation from exploitation as well as abuse. For example, in the area of sexual expression, an approach that maximized autonomy but minimized protection might subject those with mental retardation to sexual abuse or rape. On the other hand, an approach that maximized protection and minimized autonomy might protect the person from sexual abuse but would deny the person's right to consent to a sexual relationship (Denno, 1997). A balance must be struck between autonomy and protection.

A certain structure can be applied when making decisions to honor a choice or consent given by a person with mental retardation. (For the importance of choice in the lives of people with mental retardation, see Sundram, et al., 1994; Terrill & Rowitz, 1991.) Highest scrutiny should be given to high-risk decisions that are unclear or inconsistent with a person's known values and interests. Lowest scrutiny should be applied to low-risk decisions that are clear or consistent with a person's known values and interests. Moderate scrutiny should be give to high-risk decisions that are consistent with a person's known values or to low-risk decisions that are inconsistent with known values (Sundram, pp. 3–16). The increasing importance of both consent and choice in the mental retardation field is reflected in the careful and balanced approach to the issues discussed in the remainder of the *Guide to Consent.*

References

Denno, D. (1997). Sexuality, rape, and mental retardation. *University of Illinois Law Review, 1997*(2), 315–434.

Dinerstein, R. (1990). Client-centered counseling: Reappraisal and refinement. *Arizona Law Review, 32,* 501–604.

Ellis, J. (1992). Decisions by and for people with mental retardation: Balancing considerations of autonomy and protection. *Villanova Law Review, 37,* 1779–1809.

Sundram, C. et al., (Ed.). (1994). *Choice & responsibility: Legal and ethical dilemmas in services for persons with mental disabilities.* Albany, NY: NYS Commission on Quality of Care for the Mentally Disabled.

Sundram, C. (1994). A framework for thinking about choice in responsibility. In C. Sundram (Ed.), *Choice & responsibility: Legal and ethical dilemmas in services for persons with mental disabilities* (pp. 3–16). Albany, NY: NYS Commission on Quality of Care for the Mentally Disabled.

Superintendent of Belchertown State School v. Saikewicz, 370 N.E.2d 417 (Mass. 1977).

Terrill, C. F., & Rowitz, L. (1991). Choices. *Mental Retardation, 29,* 63-64.

Turnbull, H. R. III. (Ed.). (1977). *Consent handbook.* Washington, DC: American Association on Mental Deficiency.

CHAPTER 2

Adult Guardianship and Alternatives

■

Joan L. O'Sullivan
University of Maryland School of Law

This *Guide to Consent* generally addresses the subject of consent, the ability of persons with mental retardation or other developmental disabilities to consent to matters that significantly affect their life or property. Guardianship concerns the inability of a person to give knowing consent, either totally, partially, or temporarily. Guardianship is a court action in which someone alleges that the person with disabilities *cannot* consent.

Whether or not to seek guardianship of a person with developmental disabilities is a perplexing question for family members, service providers, and the state alike. It embodies the conflict with which many struggle: the tension between the impulse, on the one hand, to protect the person from harm and bad decisions, and the desire, on the other hand, to preserve the person's autonomy, to allow the person to achieve maximum potential, and to learn from the consequences of good and bad decisions, as we all do.

Guardianship is a serious step, not to be undertaken lightly or simply because the person turns age 18 and legally is no longer a child or because an adult makes unpopular or eccentric decisions. It brings court intervention and oversight into the lives of the person and the guardian. Once granted, guardianship is difficult to undo. But sometimes guardianship is absolutely necessary and is the only answer to a serious and potentially dangerous problem.

This chapter will discuss what guardianship is and how the process works in most states. It also will consider alternatives to guardianship in detail. Alternatives to guardianship are ways to solve problems while avoiding guardianship, in order to cause the least possible intrusion into the life of the person with mental retardation or other developmental disabilities.

This chapter focuses on guardianship of adults. Parents are the natural legal guardians of minor children (until they reach 18 years of age). If the parents are absent or dead, it is sometimes necessary to petition for guardianship of a minor, but this chapter will not address that issue.

Readers should consult guardianship laws and procedures in their own states. Definitions of incompetency or incapacity differ from state to state, as do the procedures for filing a guardianship action and the effects of a guardianship.[1]

Definition of Adult Guardianship

The guardianship of an adult is a legal procedure in which a court determines that a person has severe disabilities that impair the person's ability to make decisions, that the person is in need of protection, and that there is no less restrictive alternative to guardianship. The court appoints someone else, the guardian, to act for that person and authorizes the guardian to make decisions about her person, property, or both. Some states call a guardian a conservator or a committee. Some states do not differentiate between a guardian for the person and property, but most do. One person can serve as both guardian of the person and guardian of the person's property, or different people can take each role.

Before a guardian is appointed, the law may refer to the subject of the proceedings as "the alleged disabled person." After a guardian is appointed, the person may be referred to as "the ward." In this chapter, we refer to the subject of the guardianship case as "the person," both before and after a guardian is appointed. Also,

---

[1] The terms *incompetency* and *incapacity* are often used interchangeably in law to describe an inability to perform tasks. *Incapacity* has become the preferred term, however, because it avoids the "all or nothing" implication of *incompetency* (Sabatino, 1996).

in this chapter, the feminine pronouns *she* and *her* are used to refer to the subject of the guardianship proceeding, because women are more often the subject of guardianship proceedings.

Guardianship is a way for the state to enter into the life of an adult to assure that the person's basic needs are met and that her property is protected and used for her benefit. The court acts with state authority in appointing a guardian as its agent to protect the vulnerable person.

In deciding whether a person needs a guardian, a court should consider the extent of the person's ability to make rational decisions. As with the rest of the population, those with mental retardation and other developmental disabilities have various levels of decision-making ability. To determine whether a guardianship is necessary, the court should ask what decisions must be made, whether the person has the ability to make those specific decisions, and whether there is any way the decisions can be handled without the appointment of a guardian.

Effects of Guardianship

The appointment of a guardian removes some or all of the person's ability to make decisions about her life. The court withdraws the authority and autonomy that the person has as an adult and gives it to the guardian. The guardian stands in the shoes of the person, and others look to the guardian, not to the person, for personal or financial decisions.

If a court appoints a guardian of someone's *person*, the guardian, not the person, will make decisions such as where the person is to live, what medical treatment she is to receive, who her doctors should be, with whom she should associate, or where she should travel.

A court will appoint a guardian of property if the person has substantial assets to administer. If a court appoints a guardian of *property*, the guardian, not the person, will make decisions about how, where, or when to spend the person's money or how to administer her property. Usually, all control over the person's finances and property is given to the guardian. The guardian typically collects all money due to the person and from that money pays her bills and buys her necessities. The guardian of the property can sell the person's assets and invest the proceeds as the guardian sees fit.

Other effects of guardianship differ from state to state. In some states, a person who has a guardian of her property may retain the capacity to vote, decide to marry, write a will, or make medical decisions. For example, in New Hampshire the court must specifically find which legal rights the person is incapable of exercising. Under this statute, a person who is found incapacitated and in need of a guardian retains the right to marry, to testify in any proceeding, to make a will and to contract, unless the court finds otherwise in its order (N.H. Rev. Stat. Ann. § 464-A:9 IV, 1997). In other states, however, plenary guardianships, also known as full guardianships, are the norm. When such a guardianship is granted, the person no longer can act for herself in any capacity; all authority is given to the guardian, although the guardian may have to seek court approval for major decisions.

The Need for Guardianship

Not everyone with a mental disability needs a guardian. It is seldom necessary to seek guardianship for someone with mental retardation simply because the person reaches 18 or 21. A decision about guardianship should be based on the person's strengths and weaknesses and the available support network.

There are many ways to handle the affairs of a person with disabilities without resorting to guardianship. For example, relatives and friends may continue to support and care for the person without court intervention. The person with disabilities may have the capacity to sign a durable power of attorney for her financial affairs. She may have the ability to make some medical decisions for herself and to delegate more complicated decisions to individuals she trusts by using a durable power of attorney for health care.

Because guardianship is such an invasive procedure and has such long-lasting consequences for the person with disabilities, it is best to seek alternatives if at all possible. We discuss many alternatives to guardianship later in this chapter.

Reasons to Avoid Guardianship

The most important reason to avoid guardianship is that it is a measure that deprives a person of control of her own life. An adult under guardianship usually has no authority to make legally binding decisions. The guardianship order may be so broad that it deprives the person of far more rights than necessary to solve the problem at hand. For many people under guardianship, this deprivation has little or no meaning, because they have such limited ability to comprehend. But for others, especially those who are working hard to achieve independence, it can have a devastating effect, because they have been deprived of all autonomy. Guardianship conveys a strong message of *inability* to those with mental retardation and other developmental disabilities. It may create antagonism between the person and the guardian, as the person is thwarted in her efforts to make her own decisions and to learn from their consequences (e.g., *In re M. R.*, 1994).

The late United States Congressman Claude Pepper (D-FL), a leader in championing the rights of older people and other vulnerable groups, said the following when considering the effects of a guardian on the life of a person with disabilities (here called "the ward"):

> The typical ward has fewer rights than the typical convicted felon—they no longer receive money or pay their bills. They cannot marry or divorce. By appointing a guardian, the court entrusts to someone else the power to choose where they live, what medical treatment they will get and, in rare cases, when they will die. It is, in one short sentence, the most punitive civil penalty that can be levied against an American citizen, with the exception, of course, of the death penalty (Abuses in Guardianship, 1987).

Another reason to avoid guardianship is that it brings—some would say entangles—the court in the life of the person. This involvement can result in complications, time delays, and unnecessary legal expense. In many states, the guardian of the property must file yearly financial reports with the court. Filing may prove to be an overwhelming task for some family members, but failure to do so may result in being removed as guardian and replaced by someone else. In other instances, the guardian may have to seek approval of the court before the guardian can make medical and other personal decisions for the person. In many states, if the family member were not a guardian, he or she would have the authority to make medical decisions, without court intervention, after consultation with the person's health care providers.

Guardianship can be expensive. In most states, the person requesting a guardianship, called the petitioner, must hire an attorney to draft the papers and file them in the court. Another attorney usually is appointed by the court to represent the subject of the case. The petitioner must pay a filing fee with the court, although the fee may be waived if the petitioner is indigent. In addition, the guardian of the property may charge a yearly fee for handling the person's finances.

Finally, filing for guardianship can be time consuming. Unless a life-threatening emergency exists, the petitioner will have to file with the petition a physician's or psychologist's evaluation or certification of the person's incapacity. In addition, the length of the judicial process varies from state to state, but it may take 2 to 6 months or even longer to appoint a guardian. This time period may be too long to resolve the immediate problem.

In many states, the guardianship law states that a guardian should be appointed only if there is no less-restrictive alternative. Sometimes there *is* no alternative to guardianship. It may be the only way to protect someone who cannot protect herself. But guardianship should be a last resort, after every other solution has been tried and has failed (Kapp, 1996).

Determining Capacity and Incapacity

The person asking for guardianship must prove that the subject of the proceedings is unable to make her own decisions and is mentally incapacitated. Mental *incapacity* generally means that a person has impaired or very limited ability to reason, remember, make choices, see the consequences of actions, and plan for the future. In law, it means that the person is unable to make legally binding decisions. *Incompetency* is another word frequently used to indicate a person's inability to make decisions for him- or herself. Although the terms are often used interchangeably, *incompetency* suggests a more global inability.

There is no bright line dividing those who are competent from those who are not. A person can be competent to make some decisions but not others. For example, a person may be able to express her opinion about whom she trusts to handle her money but may not be able to manage a bank account or fill out an income tax form. She may be able to decide she wants a flu shot but not be able to decide which treatment is best for her breast cancer.

The law presumes that all adults have mental capacity until proven otherwise. Until a person has been found to be incapacitated by a judge in a guardianship proceeding, or according to another law regarding capacity, that person is assumed to be competent and has the right to make her own decisions. A person's mental retardation does not automatically mean that the person is mentally incompetent. Many people with mental retardation have the capacity to make decisions and to handle their own money.

When a guardianship case is filed against a person, a judge will decide if that person is legally incapacitated. The judge must be persuaded that the person's everyday decision-making ability is severely impaired, that the person lacks sufficient understanding or capacity to make responsible decisions, and that there is no other less drastic alternative to appointing a guardian. The judge will consider particularly whether the person can make informed decisions about personal care, food, shelter, and medical care or about property, money, and finances.

Incapacity is defined differently in different states. Some states use a diagnostic definition of incapacity, in which merely having a diagnosis of mental retardation is enough, along with evidence that the person is not able to take proper care of herself, to convince a judge to order guardianship. Newer statutes define incapacity according to the functions the person can and cannot do, which gives the judge more guidance in determining the assistance the person needs from a guardian, without imposing unnecessary restrictions on the person's autonomy. (See N.H. Rev. Stat. Ann. § 464-A:2 XI, 1997: "'Incapacity' means a legal, not a medical, disability and shall be measured by functional limitations. It shall be construed to mean or refer to any person who has suffered, is suffering or is likely to suffer substantial harm due to an inability to provide for his personal needs for food, clothing, shelter, health care or safety or an inability to manage his or her property or financial affairs. Inability to provide for personal needs or to manage property shall be evidenced by acts or occurrences, or statements which strongly indicate imminent acts or occurrences....Isolated instances of simple negligence or improvidence, lack of resources or any act, occurrence or statement if that act...is the product of an informed judgment shall not constitute evidence of inability to provide for personal needs or to manage property.") Readers should research their own state laws when deciding whether a person with mental retardation or other disabilities meets their state's definition of incapacity (Tor & Sales, 1996).

In most states, physician certificates of incapacity must be filed with the petition for guardianship. In some states the certificates may be completed by licensed psychologists. The certificate usually verifies that the person is unable to make or communicate responsible decisions about her person or property. It may list the person's mental and physical diagnoses, the prognosis for recovery, and the expected duration of the disability.

Tests for Mental Capacity

To certify incapacity, physicians or psychologists must examine and test the person. (Some states require certification of incapacity only by medical doctors; others permit psychologists to file certificates as well; see e.g., Ga. Code § 29-5-6, 1997; Wash. Rev. Code § 11.88.045 (4), 1997; Wis. Stat. Ann. § 880.33, 1997.) Professionals test for mental capacity through the use of psychological tests, mental status examinations, in-depth neuropsychological examinations, scales for depression, and measures of the person's functional ability to perform the activities of daily living, such as dressing, eating, and bathing. In evaluating those with mental retardation, the examiner should administer tests for intellectual functioning and adaptive skills. The AAMR definition of mental retardation is helpful in diagnosing mental retardation. The AAMR (1992, p. 5) defines mental retardation as

> ...substantial limitations in present functioning. It is characterized by significantly subaverage intellectual functioning, existing concurrently with related limitations in two or more of the following applicable adaptive skill areas: communication, self-care, home living, social skills, community use, self-direction, health and safety, functional academics, leisure and work. Mental retardation manifests itself before age 18.

But the AAMR definition does not establish a standard for determining when a person with mental retardation is or is not competent to act on his or her own behalf. That determination must be made by the court and should include evidence from experts and from those close to the person who can testify about the person's abilities as well as limitations. In determining whether guardianship is appropriate, the court should consider the extent to which the limitations create a need for the protection of the person. The court should tailor any guardianship order to take into account the person's strengths as well as limitations.

Once the testing is complete, the evaluator makes a clinical judgment about the person's mental capacity and completes the certificate of incapacity that is filed in the guardianship case. The certificate may become part of the evidence in the case, or the certificate's author may be called to testify.

Appointment of a Guardian

Often there is no way to avoid a guardianship action. Perhaps all other alternatives have been tried and have failed, or perhaps the situation is one for which there is simply no other solution, such as when a person with profound mental retardation owns property that must be sold. This section describes the usual course of a guardianship action.

A guardian must be appointed by a judge in most states. The process begins when a person files a *petition* with the court, asking that the court appoint a guardian of the person, of the property (sometimes called the estate), or of both. The person who is the subject of the case may be called the alleged disabled person or the proposed ward. Generally a lawyer writes and files the petition. The petition contains all of the basic facts about the person and the reasons guardianship is needed. For example, the petition may list the name, address, age, and Social Security number of the person, and state the relationship of the petitioner to the person. It should explain why the petition is being filed and why the petitioner is asking that a guardian be appointed. It should list the names and addresses of all other interested people, that is, those who are the closest relatives of the person, as well as any agency that is paying money to her, and anyone else whom the petitioner thinks should be notified about the guardianship petition.

The petition can be filed by a close family member, friend, or public agency such as the department of social services. Sometimes service agencies for those with mental retardation file petitions for guardianship of their clients.

As discussed earlier, one or two certificates signed by health professionals are usually required to be filed with the petition. The professional certifying the disability must have examined the person and must certify that the person is incompetent. Often the first hurdle in filing for guardianship is obtaining these certificates.

The petition is filed in a court, usually in the county in which the person lives. There may be a fee to file the petition, which may be waived if the petitioner is too poor to pay it. In some states, the court will appoint an attorney to represent and advocate for the person. In others, the court will ask a court investigator or court visitor to interview the person and report to the court (sometimes called a guardian *ad litem*). The petition, the doctors' certificates, and other court papers are served, or officially delivered, on the person and her attorney if one is appointed. All of the interested people (close family members and agencies paying benefits to the person) listed in the petition are also sent a copy of the papers. The court gives these people a certain amount of time to object to the guardianship, or to otherwise communicate with the court.

Rights of the Person Alleged to Need a Guardian

The person alleged to need a guardian may defend herself against the appointment of a guardian. Sometimes there is no defense, but in other cases involving those with mental retardation, the person may feel strongly about preserving her autonomy and may work with her lawyer to defeat the guardianship petition (see e.g., *In re Boyer*, 1981; for other cases not involving mental retardation in which petitions for guardianship were rejected, see *In re Maher*, 1994; *In re Estate of Silverman,*1993; *In re Estate of Wood*, 1986). For example, the person may not like or trust the person who is asking to be named guardian. She may think the person simply wants control of her money or she may prefer a different decision maker (e.g., *In re M. R.*, 1994). Or she may argue that she can care for herself adequately and present a plan that will assure her safety. Whatever her objection, the person has the right to try to prove in court that she does not need a guardian or that particular guardian. Her lawyer is appointed to help her assert this position. The lawyer's role is to be the voice of the person in the guardianship proceeding, to help the person make the best case possible, and to be sure that she has her "day in court."

There are many things a lawyer for the person can do. The lawyer can:

- investigate to try to find less restrictive alternatives to guardianship, such as supportive services that will enable the person to remain independent;

- ask for a social work assessment of the situation to identify care options for the person;

- get another, more favorable, medical or psychological examination to counter the certificates filed by the petitioner;

- contact and subpoena potential witnesses who will support the person's position;

- find someone more acceptable as a guardian, if the person objects to the proposed guardian; and

- argue for a limited or temporary guardianship order, so that even if a guardian is appointed, the person is left with as much control over her life as possible.

In addition to the right to an attorney, the person may have these legal rights:

- the right to a jury trial;

- the right to be present in court when her case is heard if she so chooses;

- the right to have the proceeding moved to an accessible location if a disability prevents her from going to the courthouse;

- the right to present evidence and witnesses;

- the right to testify in court;

- the right to ask the judge to seal or close the courtroom so that she is not embarrassed by public testimony about her mental competence; and

- the right to appeal to a higher court if the court issues an unfavorable decision.

Court Proceedings

In most cases, there will be a hearing before a judge on the facts presented in the petition. The judge must decide:

- Is the person incapacitated according to the legal definition?

- Is there a need for a guardian, or are there less restrictive alternatives?

- Is the proposed guardian an appropriate person to be named?

The judge will take testimony or ask for other evidence to prove these issues. Usually the petitioner testifies, as well as others who know about the case, such as social service workers. Often a health professional testifies about capacity. The person may testify as well, in order to tell the judge what she wants and thinks should be done.

A family member or friend of the person, as well as an attorney, public agency, or trust company, can serve as guardian. The court determines which individual would be the most appropriate to serve as guardian. A guardian must be willing to serve, must demonstrate a familiarity with the person and her needs, and must show that the guardian is able to meet those needs. Some states require the guardian to have formal training before taking on a guardian's duties. The guardian of property must be willing to keep records of all the financial matters handled for the person and must be able to file timely reports to the court about the person's well-being and property. The court should be aware of potential conflicts of interest, and may be reluctant to appoint a guardian who has a vested interest in the finances of the person. For example, residential service providers may not be appropriate guardians of property because they would be responsible for paying themselves from the client's funds.

Guardianship Orders

After both sides have presented their cases, the judge will make a decision. If the petitioner does not present substantial evidence that the person needs a guardian, or that there are no less-restrictive alternatives, the guardianship suit may be dismissed.

The judge will issue an order that states whether or not the person meets the legal definition of a person who needs a guardian; if so, the order designates the name of the person or agency the court appoints. The court will also state in the order exactly what powers the guardian has.

In some states, the court may give to the guardian only those powers that the petitioner has proven to be necessary. This order is called a limited guardianship order. The petitioner may request only a limited order; or the attorney for the person can argue for an order that is limited and will have the least impact on the life of the person. For example, if the reason for the guardianship is to obtain consent for a dental or medical procedure, the order may give the guardian only the authority to consent to that procedure. Provisions for limited guardianships exist in many states, but the frequency with which courts order them varies widely.

In other states, limited guardianship is not an option, and the court's order may give the guardian full control over the life and property of the person for an unlimited period of time. Guardianship orders may be modified or revoked (see below), but these changes are unusual.

Rights After Guardianship

A person may retain some individual rights after a guardian has been appointed. The extent of rights retained will depend almost entirely on how the guardianship law is written in a particular state. But by its very nature a guardianship limits a person's rights. Often, after the court finds a person is incapacitated, it may be very difficult for the person to find anyone who will take her seriously or honor her wishes. Her personal freedoms may be very limited, so that she has no spending money and little access to those who might advocate for her.

Modification or Termination of Guardianship

A guardianship ends when the person dies, or when the disability that led to the guardianship ceases to exist and the court orders that it be terminated because a guardian is no longer needed. A court may modify or reduce the powers of the guardian because the person has developed skills that she did not have when the order was issued, has recovered from the disabling condition, or now lives in a supportive environment that makes the guardianship superfluous. To modify or revoke a guardianship, the person or someone else must file a request with the court, stating the reasons for the change.

There may be additional court papers that must be filed after the guardianship is terminated. The guardian may have to file a final financial accounting with the court and a request that the court dismiss the individual as guardian.

A court can remove a guardian who cannot or does not perform the duties ordered by the court or who is acting improperly as a guardian. The person or someone on her behalf must file a motion with the court asking that a guardian be removed. In one famous case, *Guardianship of Phillip B.* (1983), the AAMR joined in an *amicus curiae* brief to urge that the court substitute a guardian for the parents of a teenager with Down syndrome who were refusing to consent to corrective heart surgery for their son.

Standards for Guardians

The guardian stands in the shoes of the person and should be guided by the wishes of the person to the greatest extent possible, consulting with her about options and decisions. If it is impossible to do so, the guardian should act in the best interests of the person. In some states, the law states that the guardian should act as a reasonable person would in a similar situation (e.g., "Degree of care and skill of guardian. In the administration of the estate and the exercise of his powers, a guardian shall exercise the care and skill of a man of ordinary prudence dealing with his own property." Md. Code Ann., Est. & Trusts § 13-212, 1997).

In 1989 three attorneys well-acquainted with guardianship proceedings in New Hampshire drafted a Model Code of Ethics for Guardians. Their purpose was to suggest ethical and legal standards to simplify the difficult decision-making process guardians must go through when making decisions for another. The authors proposed six rules for guardians:

- The guardian shall exercise extreme care and diligence when making decisions on behalf of the person. All decisions shall be made in a manner that protects the civil rights and liberties of the person and maximizes the opportunities for growth, independence, and self-reliance.

- The guardian shall exhibit the highest degree of trust and loyalty in relation to the person.

- The guardian shall ensure that the person resides in the least restrictive environment available and take the person's preferences into account.

21

- The guardian shall provide informed consent for care, treatment, and services to the person, and shall ensure that those provided are the least restrictive available.

- The guardian of the estate shall provide competent management of the property and income of the person's estate and shall exercise intelligence, prudence, and diligence. The guardian shall avoid any self-interest.

- The guardian has an obligation to seek termination or limitation of the guardianship whenever indicated (Casasanto, Simon, & Roman, 1989).

The National Guardianship Association has adopted and promoted these standards.

Responsibilities of a Guardian of the Person

The court appoints a guardian of the person to make personal decisions for the person. The guardian usually makes decisions about the person's everyday life. The court order appointing a guardian of the person should list the powers and duties given to the guardian. The duties of a guardian of the person may vary from state to state, but generally the guardian will have the authority to

- decide where the person will live;

- provide for the care, comfort, education, and social and recreational needs of the person;

- supervise the clothing, furniture, and other personal effects of the person;

- manage the funds of the person if there is no guardian of the property;

- request funds for the person's care and needs from the guardian of the property; and

- consent or withhold consent to medical care, with some limitations as explained below (see also chap. 3, "Informed Consent for Health Care").

Unless the order says otherwise, the guardian of the person can act without special permission of the court. However, there are some instances in which the guardian may have to seek special permission of the court:

- The court may have to authorize the guardian's consent or withholding of consent to medical treatment that poses a substantial risk to the life of the person with a disability. For example, a guardian might have to get court authorization to consent to major heart surgery or to refuse chemotherapy or a feeding tube for a person with a terminal illness (*Superintendent of Belchertown State School v. Saikewicz,*1977).

- The court may have to specially consider a petition to have the person sterilized (e.g., *In re Hayes,* 1980; *Wentzel v. Montgomery County General Hospital,* 1982; *In re Terwilliger,* 1982).

- The court may have to authorize a move from one type of living arrangement to another.

- The court may have to specially authorize the admission of the person to a mental institution or an institution for those with mental retardation. The guardian usually has no authority to circumvent standard involuntary admission procedures (e.g., Md. Code Ann. Est. & Trusts § 13-708(b)(2), 1997).

The court is the ultimate decision maker in guardianship cases. Thus, in the Massachusetts case of *In re R. H.* (1993), the court overruled the guardian and mother of a woman with Down syndrome who had refused to consent to renal dialysis for her daughter. Staff members successfully petitioned the court to approve the dialysis, alleging that the mother's decision was contrary to what the daughter would have wanted.

The guardian of the person may have to file an annual report with the court. When required, the report is usually due on the anniversary date of the appointment of the guardian. The report may describe the person's physical condition and living situation and describe any changes that have occurred since the last report. The guardian may also recommend whether or not the guardianship should continue.

Responsibilities of a Guardian of the Property

A guardian of the property must act as a fiduciary of the person. A fiduciary is someone who can be trusted to act in the best interest of the person. Thus, a guardian must act honestly and faithfully to preserve the person's property and to use the assets for her benefit and welfare. A guardian must use the same degree of skill and care that a reasonable individual would use in handling his or her own property.

The guardian of the property may have broad powers to handle the assets and income of the person. This power may include the authority to collect all money due to the person, such as Social Security and other benefits checks, and rent or mortgage payments.

The guardian may close bank accounts owned by the person, reopen them in the name of the guardian, and use those funds for the person's expenses. The guardian may spend the person's money to pay for housing, food, clothing, transportation, medical care, other bills the person may owe, and in general for the expenses of the person. The guardian may also make decisions about the person's property, such as whether to buy, sell, or mortgage real estate, whether to invest in stocks or bonds, and whether to borrow money to make repairs to a home.

The court may order the guardian to post a bond with the court. A bond is a kind of insurance policy that guarantees the bonding company will cover any loss resulting from the guardian's mishandling of the person's funds. The bonding company will try to recover from the guardian any losses it must pay out.

The guardian of the property usually files an inventory of all of the person's assets and income after being appointed guardian. The guardian may have to file an annual accounting one year after being appointed and annually thereafter. When the person dies or is found no longer to require a guardian, the guardian may have to file a final accounting and a petition asking the court to terminate the guardianship and the appointment as guardian.

The guardian must keep records of everything done with the person's money and property so as to file a complete accounting with the court. The accounting may contain the following:

- a description of all assets of the person and their location;

- a summary of all expenses since the last report was filed, the current balance of bank accounts, and the value of the person's assets;

- a list of all property bought or sold, and the names of the persons who bought or sold the assets; and

- a summary of all income the person received.

If the guardian of the property fails to file the required inventory or accounting, the guardian can be removed by the court and, if charging compensation for acting as guardian, will not be paid for her work (see below regarding fees for acting as guardian).

Legal Title

The guardianship estate holds legal title to the person's property and can use the property only to provide for the best interests of the person. There may be disagreement about what constitutes the person's best interests, as when the guardian tries to conserve funds rather than spending them for the current needs or desires of the person. If the guardian acts in this fashion, others may have to appeal to the court to argue for more appropriate use of the person's funds.

The guardian may make conservative investments if the person has sufficient funds for her daily needs and the money is not needed for her welfare. If the person has limited assets and income, the guardian may need a court order to invest money in instruments other than an interest-bearing checking or savings account. Generally, the guardian is held to the standard of care that the guardian would use in handling his or her own assets (e.g., Md. Code Ann. Est. & Trusts § 13-212, 1997).

The guardian may not use the property of the person to benefit the *guardian.* If the guardian uses the property for his or her own interest, the guardian may be held personally liable for the losses to the person and could be subject to criminal penalties. The guardian may not commingle the assets of the estate with his or her own personal assets.

Fees

The guardian may receive a fee paid from the assets of the person for services the guardian provides each year. The fee may be based on a percentage of the amount of income and assets in the guardianship estate (e.g., Md. Code Ann. Est. & Trusts § 14-103, 1997). Family members usually do not claim this fee, though public guardians and attorneys acting as guardians frequently do. The guardian must ask the court's approval to take a fee.

Alternatives to Guardianship

Sometimes it is absolutely necessary to seek a guardian for a person who is incompetent. In those cases, guardianship is a welcome solution to a difficult problem. In other cases, however, there may be alternative ways to solve the problem. These alternatives may not be the easiest course, nor the least expensive, but they should be tried. As discussed above, guardianship is an extremely invasive action that severely limits the autonomy of the person. It may have a negative psychological impact on the person. It is expensive and time consuming. It subjects the person and the guardian to the scrutiny of the court, and it limits the flexibility of family and caretakers. For these reasons, one should try to find creative ways to take care of the needs of the person before filing for guardianship. If there is no other solution, then guardianship is appropriate.

Alternatives to guardianship consist of a variety of legal tools, governmental benefit programs, social service or protective service programs, volunteer services, financial planning tools, and housing options that help the person with a disability solve problems relating to her person and property (e.g., Herr & Hopkins, 1994, describing a New York State program that allows panels of trained volunteers to make medical decisions for those in state institutions who have no surrogate without the necessity of filing for guardianship in court).

Advocates searching for alternatives to guardianship should start by identifying the exact problem or problems that prompted the perceived need to file for guardianship. Then they should think about alternative ways to solve those problems. For example, the problem may be that the person can no longer safely live at home. Perhaps she is living safely with relatives but needs an operation and cannot give informed consent. Perhaps the doctor tells the family to file for guardianship because the person cannot remember to take her medication, or the doctor is uncertain as to who has the authority to consent to medical treatment. Perhaps the person must enter a new living situation, and someone must sign the admission contract or apply for Medicaid benefits. In none of these situations is it absolutely necessary for a guardian to be appointed, because, as discussed below, others can give the necessary consent.

Questionable Competence and Voluntary Changes

A person who has mental retardation or other developmental disabilities may well be competent enough to express her opinions about certain matters. In deciding whether the person is competent to make a particular decision, one should ask how complicated the decision is, whether it is consistent with the way the person has lived her past life, and how dangerous the consequences are. For example, a person with mental retardation may be able to execute a legally binding power of attorney. When speaking to the person, the lawyer drafting the document should see her alone to assure she is not being influenced by anyone else. The lawyer may have to make special accommodations to understand the wishes of the person. The lawyer should ask the person to explain what legal help she wants and the reasons for her actions; he/she should ask the same questions over several visits to determine if the person is consistent in her answers. Some attorneys may want to have a doctor examine the person before asking her to sign the document, or they may want to audiotape or videotape the interview to show that the person understood the consequences of her actions.

A person who is questionably competent may be able to consent to or refuse medical treatment, as this *Guide* discusses in more detail in chapter 3, "Informed Consent for Health Care."

When it is unclear whether an individual is making a rational decision, the doctor should ask whether the decision is in line with decisions the person has made in the past. The doctor may ask about the person's known beliefs, values, and patterns of behavior. For example, if the person is refusing to have an operation for cancer, the doctor should ask whether that person has a longstanding dislike of medical treatment and whether she has refused to get treatment in the past. If the refusal of treatment is new behavior for the patient, it may not be an informed decision.

When deciding whether to follow the directions of one who is questionably competent, the surrogate can also consider the seriousness of the decision. If the results of the decision are not clearly and directly linked to an immediate danger, then the person's decision may be followed. For example, a decision about whether to have a flu shot may be left up to a questionably competent person, while a decision about whether to have an emergency operation for appendicitis may not be.

If a family member or friend can convince the person to *voluntarily* change a decision, there is no need to file for guardianship. This solution is perhaps the easiest of the alternatives to guardianship. For example, if the person will voluntarily leave her home and go to a new situation, there is no need to file for guardianship. If the person does not protest the change or willingly accepts the services that someone arranges for her, the problem is solved. It is unnecessary to seek the court's approval to make this change, unless the person protests or resists. One should not use undue influence to achieve this level of cooperation, however, or lightly seek to override the preferences of one with disabilities.

Consent to Medical Care

One of the most common reasons for people to file for guardianship is to authorize medical treatment for a person who cannot understand or consent to the treatment herself. Doctors and other health professionals must have a patient's *informed consent* before giving medical treatment. Informed consent means that before a physician can treat a patient, the doctor must explain the pros and cons of and the alternatives to the treatment. The patient must agree to be treated, unless the situation is an emergency. The patient must understand the nature of the treatment, the dangers and possible side effects of the treatment, and must give consent freely, without pressure to do so (see also chap. 3).

If a person cannot understand the doctor's explanation, the doctor must obtain informed consent from someone else. That person may be a guardian, but may also be a family member or friend acting as a health care agent or under a state's surrogate decision-making laws (e.g., Ill. Rev. Stat. ch. 755 § 40/25, 1997; Md. Code Ann., Health-Gen. § 5-605, 1997).

A person with mental retardation or other developmental disabilities may have sufficient capacity to appoint a trusted relative or friend to make medical decisions in an advance directive (also called a living will or power of attorney for health care).

If the person cannot appoint a health care agent, a surrogate decision maker may consent to medical care. A surrogate is a substitute, or proxy, who acts for the person. State laws generally set out the circumstances under which someone else can make medical decisions for a person who is unable to understand the issues (e.g., Del. Code Ann. tit.16 § 2507, 1997; Ill. Rev. Stat. ch. 755 § 40/20, 1997; N.M. Stat. Ann. § 24-7A-5, 1997; W.Va. Code § 16-30B-5, 1997; see also N.Y. Mental Hyg. Law § 80.07, 1997, a unique health care decision-making plan for residents of New York mental hygiene facilities who have no surrogate).

Either of these methods would allow someone else to make a medical decision for an incompetent person without having to file for guardianship.

Limitations on Surrogates

In most states, a surrogate *may not* authorize treatment

- When the patient, even if incapacitated, is actively refusing treatment. When the patient is refusing treatment, it will probably be necessary to ask that a guardian be appointed to consent to treatment. For example, the appointment of a guardian may be necessary when a person with mental retardation refuses to allow a dentist to work on the person's teeth and must be anesthetized to be treated.

- When the treatment is sterilization or treatment for a mental disorder.

Services for the Person With Disabilities

In most cases, the person or family members can consent to community or other personal services without the need for guardianship. Community residential supports and services seldom, if ever, require the consent of a guardian to begin serving a person. Most agencies first ask the person with disabilities whether she wants a particular service, and they will generally abide by that decision. They may also consult with the person and family member in making a decision. Because those serving persons with disabilities often start with the presumption that the person is competent to make a decision, they avoid the need for guardianship if at all possible (J. Pierson, executive director, ARC of Frederick County, MD, March 16, 1998).

Finances

There are several ways to manage money or property without going through the guardianship process. Some arrangements must be made with the cooperation of the person, and others can be implemented despite a person's incapacity. Some of these options are listed below.

Durable Power of Attorney

A durable power of attorney is a legal document in which one person, called the principal, appoints another person, called the agent, to act on his or her behalf. Durable simply means that the principal intends that the document will stay in effect even after the principal becomes incompetent.

A guardian of the property may not be necessary if the person writes or has written a durable power of attorney. An agent appointed in a power of attorney usually is given the same authority a guardian would have to handle all financial matters for the principal. Generally, if the person is able to execute a valid power of attorney, there will be no need for a guardian of the property.

A person must be mentally competent to write a power of attorney. Many people with mental retardation have the capacity to express adequately what they want. The person must be able to understand what property she has and the consequences of appointing an agent and be able to communicate clearly that she wants a certain person to handle her financial affairs.

Because the agent usually has broad power over the person's finances, it is important to select a trustworthy agent who is experienced in business matters. A power of attorney is not an option for someone who does not have a trusted friend or relative willing to take on the duties.

Representative Payee

Guardianship of the property may be unnecessary if the individual's income is derived mainly from Social Security, Supplemental Security Income (SSI), the Veteran's Administration, or other governmental benefits and the person has few or no assets. These agencies will appoint another person or agency to receive benefit checks for a person who is unable to handle her benefits alone. The person appointed is called the representative payee. Once appointed, the representative payee can collect the person's monthly income and use it to pay her bills.

There are many advantages to the representative payee program. The representative payee serves the same simple money management function as a guardian of the property but is not court appointed. The process is much simpler and less expensive than a guardianship. Because a court does not find the person incompetent, the person retains a sense of independence and autonomy.

The agency paying the benefits will oversee the representative payee in much the same way that the court supervises a guardian of the property. The representative payee must file an annual report with the agency, verifying that the person's funds have been spent on her needs.

Representative payees are usually family members or friends, but service providers, public agencies, and volunteer organizations can also serve as the representative payee. However, a conflict of interest could arise if the person serving as representative payee also cares for the person and takes a fee from the funds for that care. Federal law limits those who may collect a fee to community-based, nonprofit social service agencies, licensed and bonded in the state. In addition, the agency must serve at least five persons as representative payee and not be creditor of the individual. The agency must apply to the Social Security Administration (SSA) for authorization to collect a fee. Once authorized, the agency may charge the lesser of 10% of the person's monthly benefit or $25 (20 C.F.R. 404.2040a & 416.640a).

To be named a representative payee, one applies to the agency paying the benefits. A doctor must sign a medical form that certifies that the person is not able to handle her own money. This form is filed with the agency. The agency will ask if it is in the best interests of the person for a representative payee to be appointed. The agency will notify the person that someone has applied to be her representative payee. If the person does not object, the agency will send the monthly check to the representative payee, for the use of the beneficiary. The representative payee can open a bank account in both names and can pay the person's bills and buy necessities for her from the monthly income. The representative payee must always act in the best interests of the person (20 C.F.R. 404.2035 & 416.635).[2]

Banking Services

Banks can provide some money management services for those who have accounts. It may be possible to arrange for the following services:

---

[2] The representative payee system has come under criticism in the past because SSA failed to investigate potential representative payees who later misused the beneficiary's funds. Other criticism involves the failure of SSA to notify properly the beneficiary about the appointment of a representative payee and failure to demand accountability from the person handling funds. In 1995, SSA chartered the Representative Payment Advisory Committee to investigate the system and to make recommendations to improve it (see Representative Payment, Advisory Committee, 1996).

- Direct deposit: A person's regular income, such as salary or SSI benefits, can be directly deposited into the individual's account, saving her a trip to the bank.

- Direct payment: The bank can make direct payments from the individual's account for routine bills such as rent, mortgage payments, and monthly utility bills (see chap. 5, concerning the benefits of home ownership for people with disabilities). With the bank automatically paying these bills, the person is relieved of having to remember to write checks for them each month.

- Personal money managers: If the person has substantial funds, she can hire a personal money manager to receive funds and pay bills.

- Power of attorney accounts: A bank account may be opened as a power of attorney account that allows an agent to act for the owner of the account. The agent has no ownership interest in the account.

- Joint bank accounts: Joint bank accounts can prevent the need for a guardian of the property. If two or more people own a checking or savings account, all owners usually can deposit and withdraw money from that account. A person who has limited understanding may still be able willingly and knowingly to sign a bank's signature card to establish a joint account so that someone else can help her with handling money and paying bills.

There are some disadvantages to joint bank accounts. Because adding a person's name to a bank account gives that person an interest in the funds in the account, governmental benefit programs, such as Medicaid, may see this as making a prohibited gift. Medicaid may attribute ownership of all the funds in a joint account to the person applying for benefits, regardless of who owned the account originally. The funds in a joint account may be attached by the co-owner's creditors. Because all owners of a joint account have the right to withdraw all the funds, it is important to be sure co-owners are trustworthy.

Authorization of a Specific Transaction

Some states provide for a one-time transaction to transfer a specific piece of property without the appointment of a guardian of the property (e.g., Md. Code Ann., Est. & Trusts § 13-204, 1997). This procedure is useful when there is only one relatively simple financial matter to be handled. A petition is filed in the court asking for permission to perform the one transaction without the permanent appointment of a guardian. The advantage is that the case is closed once the transaction is completed. There is no permanent guardian of the property, there is no need to file a yearly accounting, and no need to file a petition to close the guardianship estate after the person dies. In addition, the person does not permanently lose her independence or broad-based rights, as in guardianship.

Trusts

A trust may be useful to avoid guardianship of the property. A trust is a legal arrangement by which one person, the grantor, gives property to another, the trustee, to hold for the benefit of a third person, the beneficiary. Because commercial trustees, such as banks and trust companies, usually charge a fee to administer the trust, this device is usually used only if there are substantial assets. For example, the parents of an adult with mental retardation decide to set up a trust for their daughter. They direct that after they both die, their money will go to a bank, the trustee, to hold for the benefit of their daughter. The bank will manage the money according to the directions the parents give. They might direct that only the interest on their money be paid periodically to the daughter or that the money be spent only for the cost of her housing. The trustee would not actually have legal ownership of the property, but would only hold it for the benefit of the daughter. The trustee could spend the funds only as the parents have directed. In the example given, because a trustee has the same authority as a guardian to collect funds and spend them for the benefit of a person who cannot act for herself, no guardian of the property would be necessary.

To establish a trust, families should consult a lawyer experienced in trusts that benefit persons with developmental disabilities. (Local ARCs, Developmental Disability Councils, and Protection and Advocacy agencies may have a list of lawyers other families have used for this purpose.) Trusts must be carefully written to satisfy the particular needs of each grantor and the beneficiary. It is important to word the trust so that it does not jeopardize the person's eligibility for public benefits, such as Medicaid or SSI (see, e.g., The Maryland Institute for Continuing Professional Education of Lawyers, Inc., 1983).

Guardians and Alternatives

A guardian may be appointed even though some of these alternatives are in place. Because the guardian stands in the shoes of the person, the guardian can take any action that the person could have taken. Thus, a guardian appointed by a court has the authority to revoke a power of attorney that the person has made in the past, to close or open bank accounts, and to apply to change a representative payee. Generally, a guardian could not revoke a trust that someone else has established for a person, although the guardian would have the authority to spend the income paid out by the trustee as the trust states.

Conclusion

Adult guardianship may be the only way to solve a problem for a person with mental retardation or other developmental disabilities. But because it is a highly intrusive action, and contrary to the effort to assist those persons to attain their highest level of functioning and self-esteem, it should be used cautiously and sparingly, and only when no less restrictive alternative exists. Once a guardianship is established, some may assume that the person will always need a guardian, thus depriving her of the opportunity to grow into autonomy. It is unusual when a guardianship is revoked or modified, and many states do not adequately monitor the actions of the guardian. For all of these reasons, guardianships should be used sparingly.

References

Abuses in Guardianship of the Elderly and Infirm: A National Disgrace. H.R. 641, Subcommittee on Health and Long-Term Care, House Special Committee on Aging, 100th Cong., 1st Sess. (Sept. 25, 1987) (Comm. Pub. 100-641).

American Association on Mental Retardation. (1992). *Mental retardation: Definition, classification, and systems of support* (9th ed.). Washington, DC: Author.

Casasanto, M. D., Simon, M., & Roman, J. (1989). A model code of ethics for guardians. *Whittier Law Review, 11,* 543.

20 C.F.R. 404.2040a and 416.640a.

20 C.F.R. 404.2035 and 416.635.

Del. Code Ann. Tit. 16 § 2507 (1997).

Ga. Code § 29-5-6 (1997).

Guardianship of Phillip B., 188 Cal. Rptr. 781 (1983).

Herr, S. S., & Hopkins, B. L. (1994). Health care decision making for persons with disabilities. *Journal of the American Medical Association, 271,* 1017–1022.

Ill. Rev. Stat. ch. 755 § 40/20, § 40/25 (1997).

In re Boyer, 636 P.2d 1085 (Utah, 1981) (judgment of incompetency regarding a 39-year-old woman with mild mental retardation set aside and case remanded).

In re Estate of Silverman, 628 N.E.2d 763 (Ill. App. 1993).

In re Estate of Wood, 533 A.2d 772 (Pa. Super. 1987).

In re Hayes, 608 P.2d 635 (Wash. 1980).

In re M. R., 638 A.2d 1274 (N.J. 1994) (contested guardianship proceeding between parents of an adult woman with mental retardation over with whom she should live).

In re Maher, 621 N.Y.S.2d 617 (1994).

In re R. H., 622 N.E.2d 1071 (Mass. App. 1993).

In re Terwilliger, 450 A.2d 1376 (Pa. Super. 1982).

Kapp, M. (1996). Alternatives to guardianship: Enhanced autonomy for diminished capacity. In M. Smyer, K. W. Schaie, & M. Kapp (Eds.), *Older adults' decision-making and the law* (pp. 182–201). New York: Springer.

Md. Code Ann., Est. & Trusts §§ 13-204, 212, 708(b)(2), 14-103 (1997).

Md. Code Ann., Health-Gen. § 5-605 (1997).

Maryland Institute for Continuing Professional Education of Lawyers, Inc. (1983). *Estate planning for families with handicapped dependents.* Baltimore: Author.

N.H. Rev. Stat. Ann. 464-A:9IV, 464-A:2XI (1997).

N.M. Stat. Ann. § 24-7A-5 (1997).

N.Y. Mental Hyg. Law § 80.07 (McKinney 1997).

Representative Payment Advisory Committee. (1996). *Final Report.* Washington, DC: U.S. Government Printing Office.

Sabatino, C. (1996). Competency: Redefining our legal fictions. In M. Smyer, K. W. Schaie, & M. Kapp (Eds.), *Older adults' decision-making and the law* (p. 2). New York: Springer.

Superintendent of Belchertown State School v. Saikewicz, 370 N.E.2d 417 (Mass. 1977).

Tor, P. B., & Sales, B. D. (1996). Guardianship for incapacitated persons. In B. D. Sales & D. W. Shuman (Eds.), *Law, mental health, and mental disorder* (pp. 203–205). Pacific Grove, CA: Brooks/Cole.

Wash. Rev. Code § 11.88.045 (4) (1997).

Wentzel v. Montgomery County General Hospital, 447 A.2d 314 (Md. 1982), *cert. denied* 459 U.S. 1147 (1983).

W.Va. Code § 16-30B-5 (1997).

Wis. Stat. Ann. § 880.33 (1997).

CHAPTER 3

Informed Consent for Health Care

■

Anne Des Noyers Hurley
Tufts–New England Medical Center

and

Joan L. O'Sullivan
University of Maryland School of Law

I nformed consent is a process of shared decision-making between the patient and the health care provider.[1] The health care provider must establish that the patient understands proposed treatments, risks, benefits, side effects, and reasonable alternatives. The health care provider may not act unless the patient is competent to consent and freely and voluntarily gives his or her consent.

Capacity to give informed consent is a fluid concept and varies with each individual and procedure proposed. For example, a particular individual may be able to give consent to routine treatment, such as a physical examination and standard laboratory tests. In this case, the invasiveness of the examination and tests and associated risks are quite low, thereby requiring very basic capacity to consent. On the other hand, if an individual has been diagnosed with breast or prostate cancer, the decision is much more complex and the risks much greater. The range of treatments is wide, information about mortality and morbidity

---

[1] In this chapter, we often use the word *patient* rather than *person* to refer to the person with mental retardation, because of the medical context in which the person would be seeking care or receiving services. We use the term *health care provider* to include physicians, nurse practitioners, therapists, nurses, and other health professionals who serve those with disabilities.

associated with each is quite complicated, and the response to treatment is variable, as are the side effects associated with each proposed treatment. The patient must understand current predictions about survival with or without each treatment. In this case, capacity to give consent requires a higher level of cognitive skills than in the first example.

The Process of Informed Consent for People With Mental Retardation

Health care providers must obtain informed consent through verbal dialogue and, at times, through written consent forms. Persons with mental retardation may require altered and extensive modifications to typical informed consent procedures, such as the use of augmentative communication devices. All verbal communication must be tailored to the patient's cognitive level. For example, the level of vocabulary must be simple and concrete. Sentence structure must be simple. Information must be given slowly, with time provided to digest it. Ample time must be allowed to encourage questions. Practitioners must check throughout the discussions for understanding, by eliciting answers to questions, clarification, feedback, and by encouraging questions. All written materials must be prepared at a simple reading level and translated verbally to assure the patient's understanding.

Informed consent is an evolving concept. Principles of "mutual participation," trust, and cooperation are reordering the traditional doctor-patient relationship (Lidz et al., 1984). Lidz and colleagues outlined five primary categories of informed consent: (a) the technical information to be disclosed to the patient; (b) the patient's ability to understand the information; (c) the patient's understanding and how that understanding is developed; (d) the voluntariness of the patient's decision and assessment of any undue influence or coercion; and (e) the decision itself and the way in which it is made. For people with mental retardation, special consideration must be given to all five aspects of the process of obtaining informed consent.

1. Disclosing Information

The health care provider must disclose relevant information regarding the patient's condition, proposed treatments and their alternatives, risks and benefits of the procedures, and the risks if no treatment is undertaken. The health care provider is required to give this information in terms understandable to the patient but is not required to give extensive technical information. This point is extremely important with regard to persons with mental retardation. It is sometimes assumed that the technical data known by the medical staff cannot be translated in simple terms to the person who has significant cognitive impairment, but technical expertise is not required. It is only necessary that the patient have adequate information to make a decision.

Informed consent is generally obtained through verbal discussion. The health care provider explains the patient's condition, treatment options, proposed treatment, and the risks and benefits of each. The health care provider need not keep notes about each exchange, although note taking may be recommended. During all routine care (annual physical, annual dental examination, mammography, etc.), verbal discussion is considered sufficient. When the risk/benefit ratio of the treatment is quite serious, however, the patient usually signs a written document after the verbal informed consent discussion. Informed consent documents for surgical procedures and anesthesia contain extensive information, including that the health care provider has verbally explained the situation, that the patient understands it, and that the patient gives consent. The patient's signature is evidence of the patient's understanding and consent to the procedures.

Typically, written disclosure documents are highly technical, full of jargon, and difficult to understand. The information is quite dense, written to satisfy the legal system and the complex technical nature of modern medicine. For example, documents related to even minor surgical procedures typically cover numerous possible complications, including those that are quite rare. It is difficult to write a simple consent document that satisfies all relevant legal considerations. Patients frequently do not understand the full contents of the document and are surprised when a negative outcome occurs.

Most people with mental retardation are able to participate in the process of making medical decisions, if they are given sufficient time and support. They should be given very simple information about proposed procedures, such as how much pain and suffering to expect, recuperation time, and support plans during recuperation. Other considerations should include whether the patients will have trusted individuals to help them, accompany them to the hospital or office, stay with them, and make sure all goes well.

2. Questions Regarding Competency

The health care provider must make a judgment about the patient's capacity to understand the medical information for informed consent. The health care provider ordinarily makes this determination in an interview, relying on clinical skills to assess the patient's intellectual and cognitive capacity, elicit background information and history, foster a working clinical alliance between health care provider and patient, and evaluate the patient's verbal skills.

There is little scientific literature to assist the health care provider in determining the level of mental capacity needed to consent to specific procedures. The law requires the health care provider to begin, however, by assuming that all adult patients are competent, unless there is evidence to the contrary. Chapter 2 discusses in detail the presumption of competence. In an effort to develop a useful tool for assessment, a team at Johns Hopkins University School of Medicine developed a brief screening evaluation to determine capacity to give consent (Janofsky, McCarthy, & Folstein, 1992). The tool was designed specifically for assessing capacity to make medical decisions and give advance directives. The patient-subjects were presented with a short essay describing informed consent and durable power of attorney for health care. The essay was written in versions for 6th-grade, 8th-grade, and 13th-grade reading levels. Questions written at a 6th-grade level followed the essay to assess understanding. As an example of the level of information provided, the introduction to the 6th-grade version stated: "Before a doctor can do something to a patient, he must tell the patient what he is going to do." The results of using this method were contrasted with the results obtained by an individual assessment conducted by a forensic psychiatrist using a brief history of the patient, a mental status exam, and an interview.

Such an instrument is an aid to health care providers who need concrete data to determine capacity to consent to medical care. In the same way, Intelligence Quotient (IQ) tests contribute to competency assessments for persons with mental retardation. For example, a health care provider may question the ability of a person with an IQ below 50 to understand the technical language and data associated with complex medical procedures. Similarly, using the AAMR diagnostic system (1992), a person who needs extensive supports in the areas of self-care and health and safety would probably not have the cognitive capacity to give informed consent to complex medical procedures.

As a general practice, the threshold is very low to demonstrate understanding of a condition, proposed treatments, and risks and benefits. The patient does not have to understand the technical aspects of the procedures; a simple and elementary understanding by the patient is all that is required. Health care providers who are willing to give as much information as the patient requests and to take time to explain the procedures in straightforward terms will meet the standard of informed consent.

When faced with a patient who may be unable to give informed consent, the health care provider may request an evaluation, usually by a psychiatrist. The psychiatrist will interview the patient, take a history, and administer a mental status examination.

For persons with mental retardation, a thorough examination to determine legal capacity requires that a person have a full evaluation by a clinical team that includes a physician, a psychologist, and a social worker. This team should evaluate the person from several different viewpoints, including in their evaluation relevant background information and interviews with family and support staff familiar with the person. They should also interview the person regarding the issues at hand. In some cases, a formal psychological or neuropsychological assessment may be requested as additional information upon which to base the decision. In Massachusetts, for example, such a report is required by law and must be completed by a team, which signs the formal Clinical Team Report and submits it to the court (Ellard, 1996).

3. Assessing Patient Understanding

Once information is disclosed, and the health care provider is certain that the patient is capable of understanding the information, the health care provider must still ascertain that the patient understands the information conveyed about the condition and proposed procedures. Ordinarily this determination is accomplished by a verbal discussion between the patient and health care provider that indicates the patient has understood the material. The health care provider solicits questions to avoid misunderstandings and test comprehension.

The health care provider working with a patient who has mental retardation must exercise great care during this phase of informed consent. As previously noted, questions and discussion must be conducted in simple sentences, using the patient's own vocabulary, and with ample time to digest information and think about questions. The person's verbal limitations may inhibit the types of questions asked. The health care provider may tend to ask questions requiring a yes-or-no answer. However, a variety of questions should be asked in contrasting format, so that the patient does not simply give yes as a default response, either because the patient wishes to disguise lack of understanding or to appease a perceived authority figure (Edgerton, 1967).

4. Voluntariness

It is assumed that all adults are giving voluntary consent unless unusual circumstances exist, such as incarceration or institutional obligation. In some circumstances, family pressures may affect voluntariness.

However, even under ordinary circumstances, patients may feel pressured. When faced with a doctor's request to allow their children to participate in a research protocol, mothers later reported that they felt they "had no choice" (Lidz et al., 1984, p. 30). Even patients who have a good relationship with their health care provider may feel uncomfortable about not following that health care provider's advice or about refusing treatment. Similarly, patients often feel quite awkward about obtaining a second opinion.

When treating persons with mental retardation, it is even more important that the health care provider carefully assess voluntariness. The influence and opinions of support staff and family may be unduly strong. In addition, persons with mental retardation may feel disempowered, eager to please, and unable to refuse treatment offered by a health care provider. Because of these factors, the health care provider must take care to speak with the patient privately and attempt to involve the entire support network of the patient, in order to maximize the expression of differing opinions and elicit concerns about the proposed treatments.

Voluntariness is considered a major issue when the patient is hospitalized or in an institutional setting. Persons with mental retardation who live in institutional facilities may feel influenced by staff on whom they are dependent. Similarly, persons living in homes in the community, staffed apartments, or supported living may be unduly influenced by staff and their opinions.

Health care providers can overcome these difficulties by providing a framework within which the person with mental retardation is empowered to exert control and make decisions. They can:

- make a separate appointment to address the findings regarding the patient's condition and explain treatment alternatives, risks, and benefits;

- conduct this meeting in an office rather than in an examination room; and

- conduct the meeting in the presence of an independent support person, hospital ombudsman, advocate, or volunteer and allow this person to meet later with the patient to review what was discussed, elicit questions, and facilitate understanding and decision making.

5. Making the Decision

Once the health care provider has provided information, assessed competency, assured understanding, and determined voluntariness, the patient must make his or her decision. Studies of decision making have found that patients make decisions based on a variety of factors and that the specific information is typically not the deciding factor. Comfort with the health care provider, feelings about present life circumstances, perceived discomfort, and many other factors typically take priority. Decisions made by persons with mental retardation will be based on similar considerations.

Informed Consent for Persons Who Cannot Consent

A health care provider may decide that a patient is not able to give informed consent because the person cannot understand the information presented, is unable to communicate personal wishes, or is unable to voluntarily give consent. In that case, the health care provider must look to another person for informed consent. The law gives all people the right to "bodily integrity," that is, the right to control our own bodies and to accept or refuse medical treatment. When a person is unable to assert that right because of mental incapacity, the law allows someone else to exercise the right, based on what the incompetent person would have wanted (see chap. 2, "Adult Guardianship and Alternatives," for the governing legal principles).

There are several legal bases for allowing someone else to make medical decisions for a person who cannot do so. These options include advance medical directives, surrogate decision making, and guardianship. The different methods vary in the degree of restriction they impose on the person with disabilities. As always when serving those with mental retardation, the decision maker should make every effort to choose the alternative that is least restrictive. These alternatives to informed consent by the patient are discussed below, beginning with the least restrictive alternative.

Advance Medical Directives

An advance medical directive is a written or oral expression of a person's wishes about future health care. An advance directive also may be called a living will, a health care power of attorney, or a durable power of attorney for health care. An advance directive may appoint another person to make decisions for the person and/or may state what type of care the person would want in certain situations. The laws regarding advance directives vary from state to state, and one must examine the specific requirements in one's jurisdiction.

A person with mental retardation or other developmental disability may be capable of executing an advance directive even though a health care provider has decided that the person is not able to give informed consent. The decision about whom the person would trust to make medical decisions is not as complex as that involved in giving consent to major surgery, for example. Before seeking consent through more restrictive means, the health care service provider should explore the possibility that the person could execute an advance directive for health care.

Appointment of a Health Care Agent

The person making the advance directive, who is called the principal, can appoint a person, called the agent, to make health care decisions for him or her. The advance directive should state when the agent's power takes effect. Once the document takes effect, the agent has primary authority to make decisions about the person's medical care. The agent must base his or her decisions on what the patient would have wanted in the situation, if it is possible to discuss the patient's wishes. Unfortunately, recent empirical research shows that such agents often make choices that do not correspond to the wishes of the patient, but are instead based on what the agents would choose for themselves (Muncie, Magaziner, Hebel, & Warren, 1997).

Health Care Instructions

The principal may also state in an advance directive exactly what care he or she would want in a given situation. Usually the person states whether he or she would want life-sustaining treatment, such as a respirator or tube feeding, if near death or if there is no hope of recovery. The instructions may be very broad, however, and may simply state that all decisions are left up to the agent, who can use the agent's own discretion when making decisions.

Oral Directives

In some states, a person can orally appoint a health care agent and give instructions regarding treatment. This oral appointment may be the simplest way for the person with disabilities to appoint someone else to consent to or refuse treatment. State law regarding oral directives should explain the circumstances under which they must be made. In Maryland, for example, the patient must state his or her wishes in the presence of a health care provider and another person, and the doctor must write the person's instructions in the person's medical chart and sign the notation (Md. Code Ann., Health-Gen. § 5-602(d), 1997).

Surrogate Decision Making

If the person does not have an advance directive and cannot appoint a health care agent, a surrogate decision maker may be able to consent to medical care. A surrogate is a substitute, or a proxy, who makes a decision for the incompetent person, based on what that person would have wanted. Most states have laws that allow close family members and friends to consent to or to refuse treatment for a person who is unable to understand the complex issues involved in a medical decision. Subject to variations in state law, if a surrogate decision maker is available and willing to make medical decisions, it would not be necessary to appoint a guardian of the person.

Most state laws delegate surrogate decision-making authority to close relatives or friends. The state law may list those persons in order of priority, usually naming a spouse first, then adult children, then parents.

Limits of Surrogacy

Surrogate-decision-making laws enable the parents or other close relatives of a person with mental retardation to consent to routine medical treatment for the person without any court involvement. This power exists even though the person is an adult.

Problems may arise, however, when the person actively resists treatment or objects to some aspect of routine care. It is commonly reported, for example, that many persons with mental retardation refuse to cooperate with gynecological or prostate examinations. Most state laws do not allow a surrogate to consent to treatment for a person who is resisting. When the person resists, and the care is deemed necessary, as opposed to preventative or elective, the surrogate may have to petition for guardianship of the person for the purpose of consenting to the required treatment. If state law allows, the surrogate could petition for a limited guardianship order, to consent only to the care being refused, thus leaving intact the person's right to make other decisions.

State law may not allow the surrogate under any circumstances to consent to certain kinds of medical care, such as treatment for mental illness, including electroconvulsive therapy, forcible medication with antipsychotic drugs, sterilization, and abortion. For these types of care, a court or a special decision maker must make the decision. Some states, for example, have a separate statutory protocol for forcibly medicating a person in an institution. Again, state laws vary significantly here, and it is important to examine the standards in one's jurisdiction.

Standards for Surrogates

Surrogate decision makers should follow the wishes of the person for whom they are acting to the extent possible. Unless the person's wishes are unknown or unclear, the surrogate's decisions must be guided by what the person would have wanted. This approach is called substituted judgment.

This doctrine was applied to treatment for those with mental retardation in the landmark case of *Superintendent of Belchertown State School v. Saikewicz* (1977). In that case, a man with profound mental retardation developed terminal cancer. The court considered the standard that should be used to decide whether to treat aggressively the patient with chemotherapy and seek remission of the cancer or to refrain from treating him. The

Massachusetts court held that the decision about treatment should be one the patient would make if he were competent. Several factors on both sides of the question would be considered. Those factors favoring chemotherapy included the fact that most people would choose chemotherapy and the chance for a longer life. The court stated that "[T]he chance of a longer life carries the same weight for [the patient] as for any other person, the value of life under the law having no relation to intelligence or social position." Some elements weighing against chemotherapy are common to all patients: the patient's age, the probable side effects, the low chance of producing remission, and the certainty of the treatment causing immediate suffering. Those particularly relating to the patient's mental retardation included his inability to cooperate with the treatment, the probable necessity of restraining him during treatment, and his inability to comprehend the benefits of the treatment as the reason for the disruption of his stable environment. The court specifically rejected any weighing of the quality of the patient's life as a factor in the decision making process *(Superintendent of Belchertown State School v. Saikewicz*, at 431–432).

Many states have enacted into law the substituted judgment standard *Saikewicz* established. While the specifics in each state will differ somewhat, these are some common factors that the surrogate may take into account when deciding about care for a person who is incapacitated:

- the person's current diagnosis and prognosis;

- the person's expressed preference regarding the treatment at issue;

- the person's relevant religious or personal beliefs;

- the person's behavior and attitude toward medical treatment;

- the person's attitude toward a similar treatment for another individual; and

- the person's expressed concerns about the effects of his or her illness and treatment on family or friends.

Another recent case highlighted the importance courts place on substituted judgment. A 33-year-old woman with Down syndrome was found to have serious renal disease and needed dialysis to prevent her premature death. Her guardian, her mother, decided against dialysis, but concerned support personnel asked the court to determine what the patient would want. They successfully argued that the patient had demonstrated in every way her will to live a long life, and that she desired to undergo dialysis. The state appeals court overruled the mother's decision, finding that the decision about dialysis should be based on what the patient herself would want, not on what the mother had decided for her (*In re R. H.,* 1993).

Sometimes the person's wishes are totally unknown or unclear, as in the case of someone who has had profound mental retardation all of his or her life. A surrogate must then decide based on the person's *best interests.* The "best interests" test balances the benefits of treating or not treating the person against the burdens of doing so. State laws may vary, but, in general, when deciding what is in the best interests of the person, the surrogate may consider:

- the effects of the treatment on the physical, emotional, and mental functions of the person;

- the physical pain that the person would suffer from the treatment or from the withholding or withdrawal of the treatment;

- the humiliation, loss of dignity, and dependency the person is suffering as a result of the condition or as a result of the treatment;

- the effect the treatment would have on the life expectancy of the person;

- the person's potential for recovery, with the treatment and without the treatment; and

- the risks, side effects, and benefits of the treatment.

Some laws specify that a surrogate deciding about life-sustaining treatment for another *may not* consider that person's preexisting, long-term mental or physical disability, or the person's economic disadvantage. In these states, advocates for those with disabilities and poor people have been successful in assuring that surrogacy laws are not used to judge the quality of a person's life and prematurely end it.

Guardianship

When the person is unable to give consent, is unable to give an advance directive, and no surrogate is available to consent for the person, consent to medical care must come from a court. (For a more complete discussion of guardianship, see also chap. 2.) A petitioner must file a request for guardianship of the person with the court, or otherwise bring to the attention of the court the need for a medical decision. The petitioner must present evidence that the person is incompetent (or lacks capacity) and evidence about the medical treatment needed. This evidence would center on the factors listed above, such as the diagnosis, the prognosis with and without the treatment at issue, and the burdens and benefits to the patient. If there is no one close to the person to act as guardian, the court will appoint a public agency or perhaps an attorney to act as guardian. The guardian stands in the place of the person and must act in the best interests of the person.

In some states, it is possible to ask the court for a limited guardianship, which may concern only the medical treatment recommended. For example, if the person needs extensive dental work, the guardianship might remain in place only until the treatment is completed. Limited guardianship is the least restrictive form of intervention and limits the intrusion of the court into the life of the person with disabilities. In other instances, however, the need for a guardian to consent to a specific medical treatment may prompt the court to appoint a guardian who has full decision-making authority over the life of the person. Courts often reason that medical needs may arise again in the future, and it would be inefficient to hear each case as it occurs. Attorneys appointed to represent people with mental retardation can argue against this broad-brush deprivation of rights and advocate for the most limited order possible.

A guardian of the person usually has broad authority to make medical decisions for the person but may have to return to court if the treatment at issue is life threatening or if there is a question of refusal or withdrawal of life-sustaining treatment. This requirement differs from state to state.

Treatment Without Consent

In cases of life-threatening emergency, most states authorize health care providers to act without the consent of the patient or any surrogate. An emergency may be defined as a situation in which there is substantial risk of death or immediate and serious harm to the patient and the life or health of the patient would be affected adversely by delaying treatment to obtain consent. Treatment without consent should occur only in the most emergent situations. Once the crisis has passed, health care providers must make every effort to obtain informed consent.

All too often, however, when there is no one to consent and no one to file for guardianship, the person either goes without treatment until the situation becomes an emergency or treatment is given without informed consent. Vigilance is needed to avoid either of these situations, which can place both patient and health care providers at risk.

End-of-Life Treatment

The last 25 years have seen great strides in surrogate decision making. In 1976, the parents of Karen Ann Quinlan were allowed to disconnect the ventilator from their daughter who was in a persistent vegetative state *(In re Karen Quinlan)*. In 1993, the parents of Nancy Cruzan, also in a persistent vegetative state, were allowed to disconnect the feeding tube keeping her alive (see *Cruzan v. Director, Missouri Department of Health* (1990)).

To some, this development does not represent progress. They fear that society may eventually allow surrogates to end the lives of those whom society values less than others, specifically the poor, the elderly, and those with disabilities. In the debate over physician-assisted suicide, opponents have argued that to allow this option for one group, the terminally ill, will inevitably lead to approval of euthanasia for disfavored groups.

However, in two 1997 cases finding no constitutional right to physician assistance in dying, the Supreme Court emphasized the need for protection of vulnerable groups. Chief Justice Rehnquist wrote that the state has an interest in protecting the poor, the elderly, and disabled persons from neglect, abuse and mistakes. He noted that the Court had recognized in *Cruzan v. Director, Missouri Department of Health* (1990) the "real risk of subtle coercion and undue influence in end-of-life situations." He continued:

> The State's interest here goes beyond protecting the vulnerable from coercion; it extends to protecting disabled and terminally ill people from prejudice, negative stereotypes and "societal indifference"...[Washington] State's assisted-suicide ban reflects and reinforces its policy that the lives of termi-nally ill, disabled, and elderly people must be no less valued than the lives of the young and healthy, and that a seriously disabled person's suicidal impulses should be interpreted and treated the same way as anyone else's (*Washington v. Glucksberg,* at 2273, citations omitted).

The Court left it to each state to decide its own policy on physician-assisted suicide. In Oregon, voters have approved a law allowing assistance in dying for terminally ill patients who are not depressed and who make an informed request for drugs to end their suffering. Advocates for those with disabilities should be aware of efforts to legalize physician-assisted suicide in their states and should work to assure that any such legisla-tion protects the lives of vulnerable populations.

Conclusion

Informed consent to medical treatment for a person with dis-abilities can be an ethical quagmire. The health care provider must make a careful analysis of the patient's ability to under-stand and the patient's motives for granting consent. If the health care provider determines that the person cannot give informed consent, a number of options are available to obtain consent from an agent or surrogate. As a last resort, the court may appoint a guardian to make these important decisions.

References

American Association on Mental Retardation. (1992). *Mental retardation: Definition, classification, and systems of support* (9th ed.). Washington, DC: Author.

Cruzan v. Director, Missouri Department of Health, 497 U.S. 261 (1990).

Edgerton, R. B. (1967). The cloak of competence: Stigma in the lives of the mentally retarded. Berkeley/Los Angeles: University of California Press (a classic sociological study of people with mental retardation who find various ways to "pass" as not having retardation).

Ellard, A. (1996). *Handbook on guardianship, substituted judgment, and health care proxy.* (Boston: MA Department of Mental Retardation, Metro Boston Region).

In re Karen Quinlan, 355 A.2d 647 (N.J. 1976).

In re R. H., 622 N.E.2d 1071 (Mass. App. 1993).

Janofsky, J. S., McCarthy, R. J., & Folstein, M. F. (1992). The Hopkins competency assessment test: A brief method for evaluating patient's capacity to give informed consent. *Hospital and Community Psychiatry, 43,* 132–136.

Lidz, C. W., Meisel, A., Zerubavel, E., Carter, M., Sestak, R. M., & Roth, L. H. (1984). *Informed consent: A study of decision making in psychiatry.* New York: Guilford Press.

Md. Code Ann., Health-Gen. § 5-602(d) (1997).

Muncie, H. L., Jr., Magaziner, J., Hebel, J. R., & Warren, J. (1997). Proxy's decisions about clinical research participation for their charges. *Journal of American Geriatric Society, 45,* 929–933.

Superintendent of Belchertown State School v. Saikewicz, 370 N.E.2d 417 (Mass. 1977).

Washington v. Glucksberg, 117 S.Ct. 2258 (1997).

CHAPTER 4

Consent to Sexual Activity

■

Paul F. Stavis
*New York State Commission on Quality of Care
for the Mentally Disabled*

and

Leslie W. Walker-Hirsch
Moonstone Group Sexuality Service

T his chapter focuses on how to determine when an individual is capable, legally and clinically, to consent to participate in sexual expression. It is a resource for professionals balancing the right of persons with mental retardation to engage in sexual activities and their right to be safe.

The issues surrounding consent and self-determination by persons with mental retardation create difficult conflicts for professionals. On the one hand, professionals must maintain their traditional role as protectors of the personal well-being and safety of persons with mental retardation, consistent with responsible values and an awareness of the standards of their own community. On the other hand, professionals must advocate for the right of each individual to exercise choices about his or her own life to the extent the individual can do so. Nowhere is this conflict more difficult than when it is applied to the ability to give or withhold consent for sexual expression and activities.

Historical Perspective

Sexual mores, attitudes and behaviors have changed dramatically in recent history. New constitutional interpretations and new state laws reflect these changes. Sex education and awareness is now a part of most school curricula.

Attitudes about sexual expression and activity of persons with mental retardation have changed as well. Sexual activity among persons with mental retardation is more accepted as appropriate behavior that can enhance a person's quality of life (Hayman, 1990). This view places high value on personal choice by persons with mental retardation.

Treatment philosophy in the past ignored sexual expression as an appropriate outlet for those with mental retardation or developmental disabilities. An inflexible IQ-based test was often the sole criterion for determining ability to engage in sexual activity (Schwier, 1994). This traditional concept of competency to consent to sexual activity is outmoded.

Today the right to consent to sexual activity is considered an integral part of a proper treatment philosophy that takes into account concepts of personal autonomy, free will, choice, and individual freedom. It is one of the defining indicators of adulthood and an important aspect of most people's happiness. The Declaration of Independence provides that people may define and pursue happiness in the manner they see fit, within the law and with respect for the rights of others. The United States Supreme Court has interpreted the Constitution to mean that a fundamental, general "right of privacy" exists within the Bill of Rights, and that this right protects individual choice on issues of family, contraception, procreation, and marriage (*Griswold v. Connecticut*, 1965; *Eisenstadt v. Baird*, 1972; *Roe v. Wade*, 1973; *Carey v. Population Services International*, 1977). Courts have further found, in cases concerning sterilization, that there must be a balance between protection from abuse and access to sterilization as birth control (see generally *Skinner v. Oklahoma*, 1942; *In re Grady*, 1981; *In re Nilsson, 1983;* compare *Buck v. Bell*, 1927).

Professionals serving those with mental retardation and other developmental disabilities are faced with the daunting task of writing sexual expression policies that both protect their clients from harm and recognize their right to express themselves sexually. The last decade has ushered in a socially inclusive model of service delivery for people with disabilities. Contemporary treatment philosophy seeks to advance each person's ability to function safely and responsibly at the person's highest level of independence. The American Association on Mental Retardation's (AAMR) redefinition of mental retardation emphasizes that one should consider the individual's ability to manage the complex and conflicting demands of a specific environment when deciding what degree of support to give that person (AAMR, 1992). The goal is to assist the person to move toward more independence and improved functioning, which leads to more opportunity and more lifestyle choices. This inclusive model operates with a partnership among the person, family members, and professionals that recognizes the person's character and attitudes and increases the quality of the person's life.

The trend toward greater inclusion in the community will naturally stimulate the person's desire to participate in the variety of relationships that a society has to offer, including sexual relationships. Yet while we move toward greater autonomy and responsibility in this area, we should not forget that protection from harm is one of the fundamental rationales for the professional and service relationship.

Legal Perspective

The principles of autonomy and consent to sexual activity can generally be found in state laws, agency regulations, and agency policy. Statutory definitions of consent or capacity to consent to sexual activity vary widely from state to state, from strict to moderate to liberal tests for consent (Sundram & Stavis, 1993).

For example, New Jersey and New York laws differ in their definitions of capacity to consent. The New Jersey definition of capacity to consent requires that the person understand the physiological nature of the sexual act under consideration and consent to the activity. However, New Jersey law does not require the person to understand the "moral nature" of the act, as does the New York law (N.Y. CLS Penal §§ 130.00(5), 130.05(2)(b), and 130.05(3), 1997; see *People v. Easley*, 1977).

The New Jersey statute was interpreted in a highly publicized case in which four Glen Ridge, New Jersey, high school athletes were convicted of conspiring to lure a female classmate with mental retardation into a basement and inducing her to perform sexual acts (Manegold, 1993; Oliver & Hoffmann, 1993; Hanley, 1997). In this case, the court upheld convictions for sexual assault, finding sufficient evidence to show that the victim did not understand that she could refuse to participate in the activity simply by saying no (*New Jersey v. Scherzer,* 1997).

Thus, state law can greatly influence the balance between freedom to engage in sexual activities and protection from sexual exploitation and harm. Despite differences in state law, however, there are common principles that apply to all program policies.

The first and most important task for programs serving those with disabilities is to put in writing meaningful guidelines, policies, and practices. The goal should be to strike a reasonable balance between a person's sexual expression and fulfillment and reasonable protection from harm. The policies should give explicit guidance, directing support professionals or staff concerning sexual consent.

Program policies should recognize rights of sexual privacy related to mutual, intimate activities by consenting adults, and not only those involving marriage, family, and procreation. They should provide for adequate protection from harm (Lumley & Miltenberger, 1997) and education, where appropriate, and should promote the exercise of personal freedoms for persons with developmental disabilities, including sexual rights, activities, expressions and enjoyment (Ames & Samowitz, 1995; see also Perlin, 1993–1994).

Consent for Different Sexual Activities

Knowledge, voluntariness, and consent are essential ingredients for all types of sexual contact. Persons with developmental disabilities may understand certain types of sexual contact more readily than others, and therefore may have the capacity to consent to some but not all sexual activities. We may categorize these contacts in three ways; each category has ramifications for both the legal and clinical approach to addressing the contact.

Activities Not Generally Regulated by the State

The first category consists of adult activities of a sexual nature that do not require traditional or formal legal consent. This category includes displays of affection; friendship; dancing; choice of dress; privacy in personal hygiene and sexual health services and information; masturbation or other self-stimulatory sexual activities; and access to certain erotic material. Program policies should address the person's discretion in choosing the time, place, and circumstances for those activities and observance of social protocols. Although these may involve issues of appropriateness, staff can easily assist and educate participants about them.

These acts do not depend heavily upon a person's ability to make complex judgments. As the decision making becomes more complex, the need for scrutiny is commensurately greater.

Activities Involving Mutual Agreement and Consent

The second category of sexual intimacy has some requirement for agreement and mutual consent. This category includes sexual petting, mutual masturbation, and sexual stimulation by another person. The law generally requires the clear, mutual agreement of both parties engaging in these acts. These activities may be experimental or an attempt to learn the complex human art of sexual negotiation and communication. They may help the person set the personal sexual limits of a particular relationship. Support professionals should offer guidance focused on the appropriateness of time, place, person, and mutuality, rather than on the requirements of legal or formal consent.

Activities Requiring the Highest Level of Consent

The third category covers sexual intercourse, and the greatest degree of professional scrutiny is required to determine the person's ability to consent and act safely on his or her own behalf. The professional should assess the person's understanding of the act, voluntariness, and consent. The professional must also consider state statutes, regulations, and policies of the state licensing agency. Once professionals have decided that an individual can function with reasonable safety and within the law, they must review the question of consent. Staff should monitor the person's behavior for a reasonable time and provide necessary education, guidance, and support. This monitoring will help to assure the person's safety and also verify the staff's initial decision about consent.

Qualified professionals should make at least two essential determinations. First, there should be an actual assessment of the person's ability to consent based on state law, regulation, or policy. If the decision maker has any reasonable doubts about the person's ability to consent, the decision maker should resolve them by using further testing, education, additional professional help, or a judicial determination of the person's competency.

Second, if a person is deemed unable to consent at a particular time, the provision of education, training, and other support may help the person achieve competency to consent (McCabe, 1993). An ever-increasing number of books, training programs, and consultants provide sex education for persons with disabilities and these materials should be used where appropriate. Such sources may help the persons find less intense activities more appropriate to their abilities and desires.

The professional must be mindful that capacity to give consent is not static and may fluctuate toward a greater or lesser capacity. Experience is often the best teacher, especially when it comes to human behaviors as complex as sexuality. Almost all cases will need careful professional judgment based upon program philosophies and polices that are consistent with state law, regulations, and policies.

Legal and Clinical Indicators for Consent to Sexual Activity

The most widely accepted legal criteria for valid sexual consent are knowledge (information), understanding (rationality), and voluntariness (lack of coercion) (Stavis, 1991b). Although there is some variation among these three criteria, they generally encompass the necessary considerations that the law requires. (Related competency issues can offer very useful guides and analogies in writing policies or creating testing instruments for evaluation of a client. See, e.g., Berg, Appelbaum, & Grisso, 1996.)

Professionals should include these three legal criteria in their evaluation of the capacity of a person with mental retardation or other developmental disability to participate in sexual activity for which the law requires consent (see generally, Morris, Neiderbuhl, & Mahr, 1993). Acknowledging that there can be wide variations in program philosophy and professional opinion in this field, we suggest that professionals consider whether the person:

- is an adult, as defined by state law;

- demonstrates an awareness of person, time, place, and event;

- possesses a basic knowledge of sexual activities;

- possesses the skills to participate safely in sexual activities; i.e., whether the person understands how and why to effectively use an appropriate method of birth control, and whether the person chooses to do so;

- understands the physical and legal responsibilities of pregnancy;

- is aware of sexually transmittable diseases and how to avoid them;

- demonstrates an awareness of legal implications concerning wrongful sexual behaviors (e.g., sexual assault, inappropriateness of sex with minors, exploitation, etc.);

- can identify when others' rights are infringed;

- learns that "no" from another person means to stop (i.e., understands that it is always inappropriate to have sex or engage in other activities with someone who says no or otherwise objects by words or actions);

- knows when sexual advances are appropriate as to time and place (e.g., different places and times may apply to dancing, touching, sexual intercourse, etc.);

- does not allow his or her own disability to be exploited by a partner;

- knows when both parties are agreeing to the same sexual activity;

- does not exploit another person with a lower functioning who might not be able to say no or defend oneself;

- expresses understandable responses to life experiences (i.e., can accurately report events);

- can describe the decision-making process used to make the choice to engage in sexual activity;

- demonstrates the ability to differentiate truth from fantasy and lies;

- possesses a reasoning process that includes an expression of individual values;

- can reasonably execute choices associated with a judgmental process;

- is able to identify and recognize the feelings expressed by others, both verbally and nonverbally;

- expresses emotions consistent with the actual or proposed sexual situation;

- rejects unwanted advances or intrusions to protect oneself from sexual exploitation;

- identifies and uses private areas for intimate behavior;

- is able to call for help or report unwanted advances or abuse.

Some people will never meet all of these criteria, but a person's inability to meet them does not necessarily disqualify that person from the ability to consent. Some criteria may be of less consequence in certain situations; others may suggest precautions that should be taken to assure safety or identify topics for education or training (McCabe, 1993).

Communication difficulties also may need to be overcome. Pictures, diagrams, or dolls may help communicate concepts of sexuality. In some situations, accepting gestural answers rather than verbal ones may be a perfectly valid way to verify a person's understanding.

Good record-keeping practices are essential. Staff should document the criteria they used to assess capacity or incapacity to consent. Further, they should document areas for programmatic interventions designed to teach, educate, and train the person.

A sexual relationship between an agency staff member and a person with disabilities may constitute exploitation or abuse of the person. Agencies should establish clear, unambiguous policies concerning such contact, and should assure that all employees understand the rules. Agencies would be well advised to consult state statutes, regulations, common law, and ethics guidelines for various professions, as well as their liability insurers, regarding any romantic or sexual contacts between staff and clients.

Conclusion

Sexuality is an integral part of the pursuit of happiness and self-expression. By directly addressing a person's sexuality, professionals serving those with mental retardation and other developmental disabilities can help them achieve their greatest potential. They should assess each person's ability to consent to sexual activity and, where capacity is lacking, take steps to enhance that ability. They should be knowledgeable about the laws and policies surrounding consent to sexual acts and should know the social process and standards of their community.

Professionals in the field can disseminate knowledge about responsible sexual self-determination that can inform their clients, the law, and society. There is no universal legal definition of *competency* to consent to sexual activity; rather, this concept is defined by law in each state and varies greatly among them. It is beyond the scope of this chapter to delineate all the relevant laws in each of the 50 states (Sundram & Stavis, 1994; Sundram &

Stavis, 1993; Stavis, 1991a; for a 50-state survey by a well-known jurist, see Posner & Silbaugh, 1996). But service providers do not need to reinvent the wheel in this domain. Many programs have already developed very suitable policies on sexual consent and "best practices" for implementing them. Programs lacking such policies can use these as a model for their own, taking care to seek legal advice to assure conformity with the laws of their particular state (AHRC, 1993; ARI, 1994; CLASP Homes; Heritage Centers, 1989; Developmental Disabilities Institute; Griffin, 1996; Western N.Y. Developmental Disabilities, 1996).

Even though cultural norms, professional standards, and some laws pertaining to consent for sexual activity by people with intellectual disabilities have changed dramatically in recent times, there is an ongoing need for professionals and their organizations to act as catalysts for change by supporting enlightened concepts of consent and sexuality based on practical experience with evolving standards of practice. This chapter has provided a starting point for identifying such concepts and standards.

References

AHRC. (1993). AHRC policy on sexuality. New York: Author.

American Association on Mental Retardation. (1992). *Mental retardation: Definition, classification, and systems of support* (9th ed.). Washington, DC: Author.

Ames, T. R., & Samowitz, P. (1995). Inclusionary standard for determining sexual consent for individuals with developmental disabilities. *Mental Retardation, 33,* 264.

ARI, Inc. (1994, December). *Sexuality policy and procedural handbook.* Stamford, CT: Author.

Berg, J. W., Appelbaum, P. S., & Grisso, T. (1996). Constructing competence: Formulating standards of legal competence to make medical decisions. *Rutgers Law Review, 48,* 345.

Buck v. Bell, 274 U.S. 200 (1927).

Carey v. Population Services International, 431 U.S. 678 (1977).

CLASP Homes, Inc. *Guidelines for OPS.* Westport, CT: Author.

Developmental Disabilities Institute. *Policy on assessing and supporting safe responsible sexual behavior.* Smithtown, NY: Author.

Eisenstadt v. Baird, 405 U.S. 438 (1972).

Griffin, L. K. (1996). *Informed consent, sexuality, and people with developmental disabilities: Strategies for professional decision-making.* Milwaukee: ARC Milwaukee.

Griswold v. Connecticut, 381 U.S. 479 (1965).

Hanley, R. (1997, June 30). Three men are jailed in Glen Ridge sexual assault case. *The New York Times*, p. B4.

Hayman, R. L., Jr. (1990). Presumptions of justice law, politics, and the mentally retarded parent. *Harvard Law Review, 103*, 1202.

Heritage Centers. (1989). *Policy and procedures on sexuality*. Buffalo, NY: Author.

In re Grady, 426 A.2d 467 (N.J. 1981) (establishing a rigorous procedure for the sterilization of a person with mental retardation).

In re Nilsson, 471 N.Y.S. 2d 439 (1983).

Lumley, V. A., & Miltenberger, R. G. (1997). Sexual abuse prevention for persons with mental retardation. *American Journal on Mental Retardation, 101,* 459–472.

McCabe, M. P. (1993). Sex education programs for people with mental retardation. *Mental Retardation, 31,* 377.

Manegold, C. S. (1993, March 19). Glen Ridge verdict may be milestone for retarded. *The New York Times*, p. B16.

Morris, C. D., Neiderbuhl, J. M., & Mahr, J. M. (1993). Determining the capability of individuals with mental retardation to give informed consent. *American Journal on Mental Retardation, 98,* 263–272.

New Jersey v. Scherzer et al., 694 A.2d 196 (N.J. Super. 1997).

N.Y. CLS Penal §§ 130.00(5), 130.05(2)(b), and 130.05(3) (1997).

Oliver, C., & Hoffmann, B. (1993, March 17). Glen Ridge sex jury sinks three defendants. *The New York Post*.

People v. Easley, 42 N.Y.2d 50 (1977).

Perlin, M. L. (1993–1994). Hospitalized patients and the right to sexual interaction: Beyond the last frontier? *New York University Review of Law and Social Change, 20,* 517.

Posner, R. A., & Silbaugh, K. A. (1996). *A guide to America's sex laws*. Chicago: University of Chicago Press.

Roe v. Wade, 410 U.S. 113 (1973).

Schwier, K. M. (1994). *Couples with intellectual disabilities talk about living and loving*. Bethesda, MD: Woodbine House.

Skinner v. Oklahoma, 316 U.S. 535 (1942) (overruling a sterilization statute).

Stavis, P. F. (1991a). Harmonizing the right to sexual expression and the right to protection from harm for persons with mental disability. *Journal of Sexuality and Disability, 9,* 131.

Stavis, P. F. (1991b, November/December). Sexual activity and the law of consent. *Quality Care Newsletter*.

Sundram, C. J., & Stavis, P. F. (1993). Sexual behavior and mental retardation. *Mental and Physical Disabilities Law Reporter, 17,* 448.

Sundram, C. J., & Stavis, P. F. (1994). Sexuality and mental retardation: Unmet challenges. *Mental Retardation, 32,* 255–264.

Western New York Developmental Disabilities Services Office. (1996). *Policy and procedure manual, human sexuality evaluation and training*. Buffalo: Author.

CHAPTER 5

Consent to Residential Options

■

Pam Lindsey
Tarleton State University

When people are asked to name an event that signaled their transition to adulthood, they often describe leaving their parents' home to live on their own. Adults deciding where to live give careful consideration to finances, geography, and lifestyle. Persons with mental retardation or other developmental disabilities must also consider the level of independence they are able or allowed to attain and the residential options that are available to them. Unfortunately, this group often has limited options, and a specific group or foster home may be the only choice available.

Research with persons with disabilities suggests, however, that even if there is only one viable residential option, the person who is allowed to express personal thoughts about the move will adjust to it more successfully. Therefore, it is essential that the person with mental retardation or other developmental disabilities participate to the fullest in the decision-making process. To the greatest extent possible, the person should give informed consent before a decision to make a residential move is made (Lindsey & Luckasson, 1991).

There are two compelling issues in seeking the consent of the person for a residential placement. The first concerns the person's guardianship status. The second pertains to the process itself, i.e., the steps that are involved in assuring the person's optimal involvement (Lindsey, 1994).

Guardianship and the Ethics of Discretion

Persons in residential programs typically belong to one of three guardianship statuses. First are those who have dominion over themselves: they have no guardian and can give consent to services without their authority being questioned. These persons are presumed competent under the law and are presumed able to understand the consequences of their consent, although this presumption may not be documented.

In the second group are those who have legal guardians. Program managers typically assume these persons are unable to give consent and often do not consult them about decisions. Staff seek and accept the guardian's substitute consent, without consulting the person or assessing the person's abilities.

In the third group are those who are treated as if they were under guardianship; their family members have assumed control over their affairs without the legal sanction of the courts and with little regard for the person's opinions. This assumption of control is sometimes due to financial dependence of the person with disabilities on the family. Nonetheless, this situation is perhaps the most abusive one of all, because the person has lost legal rights without due process of law. Care providers may allow the family to provide unauthorized substitute consent, thereby violating the person's civil rights.

The status of each of these groups directly affects the person's authority to consent to a housing decision. However, support professionals should evaluate each person's ability to consent on a case-by-case basis, regardless of the person's status. Staff should be careful neither to overestimate nor underestimate a person's competence, as either assumption can be damaging.

Staff should use the ethics of discretion when judging a person's ability to consent. The ethics of discretion require a good faith effort by those in authority to protect and defend the rights of members of a disenfranchised or devalued constituency. When applied to informed consent, this approach suggests that substitute consenters must consider how the person would choose, predicated as much as possible on the person's wishes and suggestions. The more intrusive the program, process, or procedure, the more discretion should be exercised by the service provider, caregiver, guardian, or parent. A residential placement decision is a highly intrusive and complex decision, because it has a dramatic impact on the quality of the person's life. Those involved should make every effort to bring the person into the process and to seek the person's opinion (Lindsey, 1996).

The Decision Process

The person's ability to consent to a housing option is measured in three domains:

- **capacity,** the person's ability to understand the consequences of the decision;

- **information,** provided in sufficient quantity and at a level and in a manner appropriate to the person's understanding, including information relating to the person's ability to financially afford and maintain the option; and

- **voluntariness,** the person's giving of consent without perceived or real coercion.

Deciding the person's level of skill or understanding to give informed consent requires a four-step, documented process.

The first step involves data collection. During this phase, the service provider or case manager gathers both formal and informal data about the person. The following facts should be documented:

- the person's intellectual capacity and strengths;

- the person's mode of communication;

- the person's personal values;

- the person's needs and personal preferences;

- the person's guardianship status;

- the person's functional ability to cook and clean; and

- the person's financial resources.

Several data sources should be consulted to cross-check the accuracy of the information. Qualitative data sources may include informal or formal interviews, observations, and conversations with the person, the care provider or family, and others who may have relevant information.

Second, the person should visit each proposed housing option to gain practical information about the living arrangement. If a group home is an option, the person should meet the staff and residents and participate in some or all of the daily routines.

Third, staff should interview the person within 5 days of the visit to discuss the person's recollection and impression of the visit. The interviewer may use a structured format, such as the Consent Screening Interview (CSI) (Lindsey, 1989; see also Lindsey & Luckasson, 1991; Lindsey, 1994), or a semistructured format developed by the staff. The interviewer should record the person's recollections of the visit, the person's capacity to understand the expectations of the proposed living arrangement, and the person's personal preferences and choices about the move. If a person is unable to recall the visit, (i.e., cannot give an account that includes an event or person from the visit), staff should arrange a second visit, followed by a second interview. The person's account does not have to be verbalized but should reflect, in the person's preferred communication style, the person's memories of the event. For example, for a person who is nonverbal or one with limited language skills, staff could use photographs of the home, staff, or other persons residing there, paired with yes or no symbols or smiling and frowning faces, to prompt a positive or negative response about the visit.

The fourth and final step in the process is the decision meeting, in which all documentation is reviewed. The person, the guardian (if any), family member or friend, a case manager, and a member of the residential program's staff should be present to discuss the benefits and challenges of the proposed move. Even those persons with legal guardians should be allowed to complete the process to assure that their preferences are considered as part of the decision procedure.

The process, when properly carried out, protects the person from being placed in precarious or intrusive living arrangements. The key to the success of the process is accurate written documentation of the person's participation in it. Documentation helps to protect service providers from legal action resulting from inappropriate placement decisions, although it is no guarantee against litigation.

Staff should review and update this process every 3 years, or more often if warranted, because some persons with mental retardation will develop more efficient decision-making skills and be able to consent with more confidence as they mature and have more opportunities to participate in significant decisions. Such persons also will learn from the consequences of their prior decisions.

Home Ownership

Owning a home is an important element of the American dream. The American Association on Mental Retardation, Legislative and Social Issues Committee, has drafted a policy statement regarding home ownership that states: "AAMR joins with people with disabilities and their families in calling for an expansion of the American Dream element of *owning one's home,* or at least controlling one's home" (1992–1993, p. 2). Home ownership can be an option for those with mental retardation and other developmental disabilities, part of the full range of opportunities and experiences available to people in this country (O'Brien, 1994). But buying real estate is a complicated procedure for most people, and it can present special hurdles for those assisting a person with disabilities. The elements of consent—capacity, knowledge, and voluntariness—should be considered in each step of the home-buying process, from the initial decision to buy to the final settlement.

Benefits of Home Ownership

Owning a home confers the same benefits on those with disabilities as on others. Those providing services to the owner must respect the values and lifestyle of the person who lives there, even if they are different from their own. The owner has more control and autonomy over his or her environment, thus enhancing independence.

Buying a home should be one consideration in developing an estate plan for those with disabilities. It may be a particularly good way for aging parents to provide for the care of an adult child after their deaths. The value of a house will often be excluded in determining a person's eligibility for public benefit programs such as Supplemental Security Income (SSI), for example, thereby enabling the person to have a secure living arrangement while remaining eligible for monthly income benefits.

Liabilities of Home Ownership

With independence comes responsibility. Arrangements for owning a home must be flexible and supportive enough to adapt to the person's changing needs and circumstances. There must be support in place to ensure that mortgage payments, taxes, insurance, and utility bills are paid regularly. The cost and responsibility of making repairs and keeping up the property also fall to the owner. Service providers can make arrangements such as automatic bill paying through a bank, or the appointment of a representative payee or an agent through a power of attorney to ensure prompt payments (see chap. 2, "Alternatives to Guardianship" subhead).

Consent to Home Ownership

To sign contracts of sale and mortgage documents, the purchaser of a home must have the capacity to understand the documents and the legal implications of the purchase and be able to take the action voluntarily. This understanding may be accomplished with the support of legal and real estate professionals. Again, those involved with the person with disabilities must make a careful assessment of the person's ability to undertake this important decision. Staff should carefully analyze data in the manner described earlier in this chapter. The person must be consulted on every decision to be certain that the decision is voluntary.

If the person is unable to understand or is incapable of consenting to purchase real estate, a substitute decision maker will be needed. An interested party may petition for guardianship of the person's property. The individual appointed as guardian of the property would then have the discretion to purchase real estate if it is in the best interests of the person and would make the best use of the person's estate. (See chap. 2 for more about the responsibilities of a guardian of the property.)

Conclusion

Choosing a place to live is a decision most people take extremely seriously. Our home and our comfort in it are essential to our sense of well-being and security. It is essential that those with disabilities have the same opportunity to make choices about where they live as others do.

The right to choose where and with whom one lives is fundamental to a person's perception of adult status. It is critical to the person's sense of independence and self-direction. Persons with mental retardation and other developmental disabilities have the right to participate to the fullest extent possible in choosing among residential options. At a minimum, persons should voice their preferences and participate in the process. They should have practical information about the benefits and challenges of the move, and staff should regard their opinions as essential to the decision process.

References

American Association on Mental Retardation. (1992–1993). *Policy statements on legislative and social issues, home ownership or control.* Washington, DC: Author.

Lindsey, P. (1989). *A study of the reliability and validity of the consent screening interview (CSI) as an assessment tool to determine the ability of persons with developmental disabilities to give direct consent for community residential placement.* Unpublished doctoral dissertation, University of New Mexico, Albuquerque.

Lindsey, P. (1994). Consent screening interview (CSI): Follow-up data. *Education and Training in Mental Retardation, 29,* 155–164.

Lindsey, P. (1996). Informed consent and adulthood: Significance in the lives of persons with mental retardation and developmental disabilities. *Education and Training in Mental Retardation, 31,* 171–175.

Lindsey, P., & Luckasson, R. (1991). Consent screening interview for community residential placement: Report on the initial pilot study data. *Mental Retardation, 29,* 119–124.

O'Brien, J. (1994). Down stairs that are never your own: Supporting people with developmental disabilities in their own homes. *Mental Retardation, 32,* 1–6.

CHAPTER 6

Capacity for and Consent to Legal Representation

■

Stanley S. Herr
University of Maryland School of Law

This chapter focuses on a topic of great importance to the self-determination and choice of clients: capacity to enter into and sustain an attorney-client relationship. This topic is important because such a relationship is the gateway to a system of justice that comprises not only the courts, but also administrative tribunals, rule-making bodies, legislatures, and many informal settings where differences are settled through mediation, negotiation, and other dispute-resolution techniques. Access to advocacy underpins the United States government's clearly announced principle of "[r]ecognizing the right of all people with mental retardation to enjoy a quality of life that promotes independence, self-determination and participation as productive members of society" (Exec. Order No. 12,994, 1996).

This chapter's discussion has three main objectives. First, it seeks to summarize applicable principles of law and public policy that govern the right of persons with mental retardation to enter into attorney-client relationships and to obtain legal help. Second, it offers a few illustrations of the types of issues encountered by persons who are either (a) relatively competent, (b) marginally competent (this category of client is also referred to as the questionably competent client; Tremblay, 1987), or (c) clearly not competent to instruct counsel. Third, it provides references and resources for further study of this technical and ethically sensitive topic.

Despite its significance, this subject has received only limited discussion in the literature of the legal and mental retardation professions. For example, the *Consent Handbook* referred to issues involving consent to representation by those of intermediate capacity as "murky," and envisioned that rapid changes in the law would require "substantial revisions" of the entire text within a few years (Turnbull, 1977, pp. v, 64). This chapter endeavors to offer a fresh conceptualization of how persons with mental retardation can give consent, assent, or otherwise be represented by an advocate. Although the primary focus here is on the attorney-client relationship, the analysis offered should generally be applicable to other advocates, such as student attorneys, paralegals, and other types of professional or volunteer advocates who seek to represent persons with mental retardation (hereinafter "persons").

Basic Principles

Access to Justice

As a matter of law and public policy, our society sets a low threshold for demonstrating a person's capacity to obtain access to advocates and thus access to the courts. For more than two decades, the fundamental right of any citizen to gain access to the courts for the vindication of rights has been recognized and strengthened for persons with mental retardation. U.S. Court of Appeals Judge Patricia M. Wald has written that because such persons are "among the most vulnerable groups in society," their right of equal access to the courts should be carefully safeguarded and they should receive "extra aid...to make that access meaningful" (1976, p. 22). Similarly, the American Bar Foundation has acknowledged that access to the courts is an "overriding concern for mentally disabled persons who wish to redress civil grievances; and such persons, like other American citizens, participate in the legal system to protect their personal and property rights" (Brakel, Parry, & Weiner, 1985, p. 436). As a result, modern laws on the right of such persons to sue or be sued are more the product of an intention to protect the rights of incompetent or marginally competent persons than any attempt to place limitations on the person's capacity to initiate the legal process (Brakel, Parry, & Weiner, p. 435).

Client-Centered Representation

Ethical rules of the legal profession (American Bar Association) (hereinafter "ABA") give strong preference to the attorney's direct representation of a person with a disability. For a client with impaired ability to make an adequately considered decision in connection with his or her representation, the lawyer must, "as far as reasonably possible, maintain a normal client-lawyer relationship with the client" (ABA, 1995, Rule 1.14). Although there are many forms of attorney-client relationships, some of the characteristics of the conventional relationship include the attorney's duties to (a) act as an agent for the client, informing the client fully and abiding by the client's decisions; (b) advocate zealously to pursue the "lawful objectives of [the] client through reasonably available means permitted by law" (ABA, 1982, DR 7-101(A)(1); ABA, 1995, Rule 1.3 and comment para.1); (c) be loyal to the client and avoid conflicts of interest that could interfere with zealous advocacy; (d) provide competent and diligent legal assistance; and (e) maintain the client's confidences (Pepe & Lindgren, 1990). These duties are consistent with a model of client-centered lawyering that encourages active client participation. To state this goal is to glimpse the ethical dilemmas and patience required to initiate and maintain a good attorney-client relationship with a client with cognitive limitations.

The legal profession's ethical rule on serving a client with disability acknowledges this complexity. It recognizes the continuum of client abilities and the need to strive for "the normal client-lawyer relationship" in the decision-making process while adapting to the client's unique circumstances and capacities. (ABA, 1995, Rule 1.14, comment 1, states: "The normal client-lawyer relationship is based on the assumption that the client, when properly advised and assisted, is capable of making decisions about important matters. When the client is a minor or suffers from a mental disorder or disability, however, maintaining the ordinary client-lawyer relationship may not be possible in all respects.") Like the normalization principle, this rule requires the lawyer to make every effort to treat the person as any other client, to communicate with the client in a clear manner, and to maximize the client's decision-making opportunities. Even if the client is legally incompetent (i.e., adjudicated so in a guardianship proceeding), the lawyer must treat the client with "attention and respect," recognizing that such a client "often has the ability to understand, deliberate upon, and reach conclusions affecting the client's own well-being" (ABA, 1995, Rule 1.14, comment). This approach is consistent with the client-centered approach that is now regarded as conventional wisdom in the legal academy as in most other parts of the legal profession (Dinerstein, 1990). In essence, the attorney has wide discretion to accept the client as a person with capacity to participate in the representation process and to fashion necessary accommodations to the client's differences and disabilities.

Some clients, however, are so impaired that the lawyer may adopt the default position of seeking some intermediary to guide the course of legal representation. The rule is permissive. It states that a lawyer *may* seek a guardian's appointment or "take other protective action...only when the lawyer reasonably believes that the client cannot adequately act in the client's own interest" (ABA, 1995, Rule 1.14(b)). Thus, the rule is contextual and leaves to the attorney's judgment whether to seek some intervention or to rely on the client's views to determine the scope, general direction, and settlement of the matter.

Less Restrictive Alternatives in Surrogate Representation

The appointment of a full guardian is generally disfavored under the dominant view in both the legal and mental retardation professions, because there are usually a number of other options for providing protective arrangements (Herr, 1995; ABA, 1989; see also chap. 2, "Adult Guardianship and Alternatives"). Indeed, the existence of a less restrictive alternative suitable to the individual's needs and circumstances is a legal bar to such an appointment (Md. Code Ann., Est. & Trusts § 13-705(b), 1997). Less restrictive alternatives include:

- the next friend: a self-appointed relative, personal friend, or concerned professional who sets goals of representation and directs the lawyer in litigation (Fed. R. Civil Procedure, Rule 17(c), 1997: A child or "incompetent person who does not have a duly appointed representative may sue by a next friend or by a guardian ad litem");

- guardian *ad litem:* a guardian for the purpose of litigation, a court-appointed limited guardian who makes legally binding decisions on the client's behalf during the course of litigation (Fed. R. Civil Procedure, Rule 17(c), 1997; Mickenberg, 1979);

- power of attorney: an agent selected by a competent client who makes decisions, including obtaining legal services, if the client later becomes incompetent or is otherwise unable to act for self;

- representative payee or protective payee: a government-agency-approved representative to manage benefit payments;

- nearest relative: parent of a minor or next of kin for an adult, who by informal custom and affinity to the client may have a related legal interest or serve as a source of concurrent or surrogate consent for the purposes of legal representation;

- self-advocate supporter or citizen advocate: a member of a client's support network who can help to empower a client to assert a civil right (Miller & Keys, 1996), validate a client's communication, or clarify a client's goals;

- protective services worker: a nonprofit or governmental agency designee whose duties can include initiating legal action such as a police investigation or obtaining legal representation for a client subject to abuse, neglect, or self-neglect through a Protection and Advocacy (P & A) office or other public agency;

- *de facto* guardian: a self-appointed defender of a client's best interests when the client is clearly incompetent, but no court has so adjudicated the client (Herr, 1989–1990 (criticizing this concept as imposing no check on paternalism and creating few incentives to furthering client autonomy); Herr, 1979; Herr, 1983);

- limited guardian: a court-appointed agent to act as surrogate in ways tailored to preserving as much of the client's decision making authority as possible;

- administrative surrogate decision maker: agency-appointed staff or volunteer who can defend a client's rights, including seeking counsel to assert a right or a claim, such as the surrogate parent program under the Individuals With Disabilities Education Act (1998) for the child without a natural parent or the surrogate program under the Willowbrook decree (*NYSARC v. Carey,* 1975, 1979) that provided *in loco parentis* representation for clients and offered a potential link to class-action counsel;

- court-appointed counsel: a lawyer appointed by order of a court in a unique individual matter (e.g., *Guardianship of Phillip B.,*1983; *Estate of C. W.,* 1994; see also Minow, 1990, pp. 343–344) or as a matter of routine in certain categories of cases such as civil commitment, criminal proceedings, guardianship, or conservatorship actions restricting the liberty of an "alleged disabled person" (Gottlich, 1995–1996); or

- representation as part of a group: class-action suit in which one or more members of a class may sue as representative parties on behalf of a class that is numerous and has common claims (Fed. R. Civil Procedure, Rule 23, 1997), or legislative or administrative advocacy.

Proceedings to obtain court appointment of counsel are generally a last resort. In the United States and abroad, it is rarely invoked (except in guardianship cases) even when the statute authorizes it (Markovits, 1996, p. 2284: "Although in all other criminal or civil cases [German] judges could order representation for parties or defendants unable to represent themselves effectively, they virtually never did so. Children and the handicapped, who needed some representation though not necessarily by an attorney, almost always were assigned social workers rather than lawyers to assist them"). Courts, however, will permit an attorney to sue as next friend when the attorney has the express permission of a minor plaintiff and there are allegations of parental abandonment (see *Child v. Beame,*1976).

Consent to Representation

At least in formal modes of legal representation, such as litigation, it is commonplace and good practice for the attorney to document the client's consent to representation. This document is known as an engagement letter or retainer. Typically it will define the parties to the agreement, the scope of the representation to be undertaken, the responsibility for paying costs and fees, the circumstances under which the representation may be terminated, and similar contractual terms. Once the lawyer is within an established relationship, whether with a client with a disability or not, this overall consent to representation will be sufficient to subsume many of the day-to-day technical decisions and logical extensions of authority the lawyer would be entitled to exercise on behalf of a client.

There may be instances in which a lawyer may act for a client despite the lack of a formal attorney-client relationship. In 1997, the American Bar Association added vital commentary to its ethics rule that permits emergency legal assistance to a person with a disability without a client-lawyer relationship having first been established. The emergency must be grave: a threat of imminent and irreparable harm to the person's "health, safety or a financial interest." The trigger for taking legal action on behalf of the person is a consultation with "the disabled person" who may not be able to "make or express considered judgments about the matter" or with another person "acting in good faith on that person's behalf" (ABA, 1995/1997, Rule 1.14, comment para. 6 (confining this authority to an emergency and where the lawyer "reasonably believes that the person has no other lawyer, agent or other representative available")). The rule is a narrow exception to customary practice, designed to maintain the status quo or avoid immediate harm while steps are taken to "regularize the relationship" with the person with a disability or put other protective solutions in place. To avoid overreaching, the lawyer would be expected to disclose this exigent relationship to any tribunal or other lawyer involved in the matter. Furthermore, the lawyer would normally be expected to forgo compensation for such emergency intervention.[1] This language fills a gap in the ethical codes where a lawyer reasonably concludes that a person with a disability who does not have an agent faces a legal emergency but "is, or appears to be, unable to make decisions on his or her own behalf—including a decision to retain a lawyer" ("ABA Report Explaining 1997 Amendment to Comment," cited in Gillers & Simon, 1998, p. 155).

There are no uniform standards or cookbook guidance to aid the lawyer in determining whether a particular client has the capacity to retain counsel. The matter is relegated in the first instance to the lawyer's reasonable professional judgment. Indeed, under the *Model Rules* commentary, the lawyer even has the option of acting as a *de facto* guardian for an apparently incompetent client who has no guardian (ABA, 1995, Rule 1.14, comment para. 2: "If the person has no guardian or legal representative, the lawyer often must act as de facto guardian"). Although commentators (Tremblay, 1987, p. 570; Herr, 1989–1990, p. 631) acknowledge the drawbacks of this approach (e.g., no public scrutiny; no independent source of guidance to, or check on, the lawyer; no guidelines for its use), it does serve as a fallback source of authority to act. However, a prudent lawyer would first want to consider all less drastic options, prepare a file memorandum documenting the reasons for action, articulate the justifications for the decision taken in terms of the client's legitimate aims or some other fundamental principles, and research the relevant laws, ethics opinions, court cases, and professional code applicable to the jurisdiction in which the client lives (Pepe, Burns, & Lindgren, 1991; ABA & BNA, 1994). For instance, state law usually determines the person's capacity to sue and the capacity to sue as a representative of another (e.g., *Developmental Disabilities Advocacy Center v. Melton,* 1982, at 285). As an ex-

---

[1] "A lawyer who acts on behalf of a disabled person in an emergency should keep the confidences of the disabled person as if dealing with a client, disclosing them only to the extent necessary to accomplish the intended protective action. The lawyer should disclose to any tribunal involved and to any other counsel involved the nature of his or her relationship with the disabled person. The lawyer should take steps to regularize the relationship or implement other protective solutions as soon as possible. Normally, a lawyer would not seek compensation for such emergency actions taken on behalf of a disabled person" (ABA, 1995/1997, Rule 1.14, para. 7).

ample, although the parent of a child with a disability will generally receive preference over an outsider's proposed representation, an unrelated next friend, guardian *ad litem,* or more distant relative may be appointed when the parent has an interest that may conflict with the interests of the minor the parent is supposed to represent (*Developmental Disabilities Advocacy Center v. Melton,* 1982, at 285). An extensive body of literature deals with the identification and resolution of such claims between parent and child (e.g., Green & Dohrn, 1996; Haralambie, 1996; Peters, 1996), and caretaker and senior citizen (Margulies, 1994; Rein, 1994; Roca, 1994; Smith, 1988).

Broad Consultation in Class Representation

Class-action litigation can raise questions of even greater complexity and controversy. Issues may arise as to whether a named party is representative of the entire class or whether the interests of dissident class members should be separately represented through their formal intervention in the judicial process. In one notable instance, the parent of the lead plaintiff in the *Pennhurst* case, in the midst of this lengthy class action, took a position on improving rather than closing the institution that diverged from the position taken by the counsel for the class (Burt, 1985). Although the court could have taken steps to have a guardian appointed for this adult child with a severe disability, the federal judge instead assumed what amounted to a *de facto* guardianship, attempting to frame substantive and procedural remedies to meet the group and individual needs of the *Pennhurst* class members and ultimately approving the terms of the final settlement as fair to the class (Burt, 1985; *Halderman v. Pennhurst State School and Hospital,* 1977, 1979; *Pennhurst State School and Hospital v. Halderman,*1984, at 94 n.2 (noting that the Pennhurst Association's motion to intervene was granted by the court below and that the Association was one of the petitioners before the Supreme Court)).

Here again a body of literature exists on recognizing and resolving conflicts between class members, between class members and their next of kin, and between members of the plaintiff camp and their counsel (Rhode, 1982; Luban, 1988; see, e.g., *Lelsz v. Kavanagh,*1983, at 1046). For instance, client-centered lawyers might consider creating "consultation groups or steering committees to obtain direction in making critical strategic decisions, especially those involving non-legal considerations" (Herr, 1989–1990, p. 636). These groups could include individuals representing a wide spectrum of affected interests, with special efforts made to identify the most articulate class members or their proxies, such as self-advocates or former institutional residents, if the class action involved an institution. Another approach to achieve the same end is to represent both an organization with standing to protect the affected individuals as well as named individual class members, as successfully occurred in *People First of Tennessee v. Clover Bottom Developmental Center* (1996). In this restructuring of the state-wide delivery of services to Tennessee's citizens with development disabilities, the parties highlighted individualization and self-determination as guiding principles in their detailed 74-page judicially enforceable consent agreement. Those principles, by analogy, offer guidance to advocates who aspire to person-centered representation. Thus, the *People First* (1996) decree states that:

> All decisions regarding services for citizens must be person-centered, driven by the individual citizens, family members, guardians, advocates, and other interested persons, and made on an individualized basis by appropriate interdisciplinary teams of competent and qualified professionals with input from those persons (at 3, para. B).

> All citizens must direct their own lives and be enabled to make meaningful choices about matters that are important to the person. Decisions about services and supports for each citizen shall be made by the citizen with the support of parents, guardians, friends and advocates (at 3-4, para. E).

Illustrations

The following illustrations are intended to show some of the contexts in which capacity for legal representation issues arise. They are suggestive rather than exhaustive of the many nuances and special issues posed by particular factual settings and legal circumstances.

Clients who can express themselves, by definition, pose the most straightforward application of the principles previously described. For instance, the majority of cases for persons with mental retardation will permit direct representation in matters such as Social Security disability benefits, appointment of an agent, execution of a will, protection of property rights, and criminal defense. This practice is consistent with the presumption of competency that, in both civil and criminal law, holds that an individual is presumed competent, absent a court's finding of incompetency. For example, if the defense lawyer, prosecutor, or judge believes that the defendant is incompetent to stand trial, a special evidentiary hearing will be held to determine if the accused can assist counsel in his own defense and has a rudimentary understanding of the underlying criminal proceeding against him (see, e.g., *Dusky v. United States,* 1960; Herr, Arons, & Wallace, 1983, pp. 27–28; for further information on the criminal justice system, see chap. 7, "Capacity and the Courts").

In the civil context, suppose a client with mild mental retardation makes the following request of a lawyer visiting an institution: "I've been working here for 40 years. Can you help me get a pension?" After clarifying the initial request through legal counseling, the lawyer could certainly proceed to interview the prospective client and to enter into a conventional attorney-client relationship to gain some form of monetary compensation for the client's decades of "institutional peonage."[2]

Mid-range cases, in contrast, may require more refined judgments in terms of legal ethics and lay assessments of cognitive capacity. Imagine a client with moderate mental retardation who needs to instruct a lawyer as to her wishes concerning living with one parent rather than the parent who is her legal guardian. This dispute and the issue of whether a 21-year-old woman with mild to moderate mental retardation had the specific capacity to decide with whom to live was decided in a landmark decision of the New Jersey Supreme Court (*In re M. R., 1994*). In a unanimous opinion, the court held that the general guardian (the

---

[2] This hypothetical is based on the claim of Charles Turner against the State of Maryland (Herr, 1987; see also Friedman, 1974).

mother in this case) had the burden of proving by clear and convincing evidence that the young woman (whose initials were coincidentally M. R.) was incompetent to make that choice. For purposes of this chapter, the court's more important ruling was that M. R's appointed counsel had the duty to advocate for her expressed preferences since "the attorney's role is not to determine whether the client is incompetent to make a decision, but to advocate the decision that the client makes" (at 1284). This conception of the attorney's role makes clear that the attorney is the agent of the person with the disability, unlike the guardian *ad litem* who is the agent of the court for the purpose of determining a litigant's best interests. However, even as the client's champion, the attorney need not advocate for decisions that are "patently absurd or that pose undue risk of harm to the client" (at 1285). The court goes on to offer the following guidelines to assist lawyers who represent marginally competent or incompetent clients:

> First, a declaration of incompetency does not deprive a developmentally-disabled person of the right to make all decisions. The primary duty of the attorney for such a person is to protect that person's rights, including the right to make decisions on specific matters. Generally, the attorney should advocate any decision made by the developmentally-disabled person. On perceiving a conflict between that person's preferences and best interests, the attorney may inform the court of the possible need for a guardian *ad litem*....Our endeavor is to respect everyone's right of self-determination, including the right of the developmentally disabled. For those who cannot exercise that right, the courts will protect their best interests (at 1285–1286; see also Robinson, 1995).

Courts and legislatures have found several ways to protect those who are plainly incapable of protecting themselves. Congress has vested Protection and Advocacy (P & A) system programs with statutory access rights to investigate incidents of abuse and neglect if the incidents are "reported to the system or if there is probable cause to believe that the incident occurred" (Developmentally Disabled Assistance & Bill of Rights Act, 1995).

Where necessary, P & A systems have successfully litigated to assist program residents who are alleged to be abused (e.g., *Alabama Disabilities Advocacy Program v. Tarwater Developmental Center,* 1995; *Maryland Disability Law Center v. Mt. Washington Pediatric Hospital,* 1995; *Mississippi Protection & Advocacy System v. Cotten,* 1991). They have sued to secure access to potential clients and their records, developing rules to visit with, speak to, and represent clients in institutions (*Developmental Disabilities Advocacy Center v. Melton,*1982; Alisberg, 1983).

Review of decisions to forgo medical treatment is another area in which courts have devised ways to permit representation of silent clients. In the early case of *Superintendent of Belchertown State School v. Saikewicz* (1977), the court appointed a lawyer as guardian *ad litem* for a client legally and factually incompetent to decide to forgo chemotherapy where the treatment for his cancer was expected to be futile and the client was expected to be traumatized by, what for him would be, unexplainable side effects. Because the 67-year-old Mr. Saikewicz had profound disabilities and very limited communication skills to convey his feelings about pain or relief from pain, the guardian *ad litem* urged, and the court adopted, a substituted-judgment test that affirmed that quality-of-life considerations should not be a criterion in similar nontreatment cases in the future (Davis, 1978, p. 451). Substituted judgment requires that the decision maker ascertain the values, interests, and subjective outlook of the person to make a decision based on what that individual would choose if competent rather than to apply an objective best-interests test.

Conclusion

Access to legal representation and to systems for resolving grievances can increase a person's leverage in achieving a measure of social and economic justice. Questions of capacity to enter into and maintain an attorney-client relationship should not become a barrier to such legal access. Indeed, modern legal systems in general, and courts specifically, have liberally construed rules of civil and criminal procedure to provide persons with mental retardation with meaningful access to representation.

One manifestation of this trend is a presumption on the part of courts, the legal profession, legislatures, and society in general that people are competent to engage counsel and otherwise participate in the attorney-client relationship (e.g., Cal. Welf. & Inst. Code § 5523(a), 1984). Although the exceptions to this presumption are not clearly defined, it would probably require the opponent to make a strong showing that the representation would be injurious to the client and to prove by clear and convincing evidence that the client lacks specific capacity to be represented. This intentionally low threshold to gain access to legal services means that, under most circumstances, courts and adversaries do not challenge individual capacity. Issues of capacity may arise, however, when more than one person is competing to be the representative of a person with a disability.

The need to clarify the roles of representative and client with a disability is ongoing. Despite two decades of steady progress, significant shortcomings remain. For instance, even when the client has capacity, some lawyers may minimize participation of their clients or relegate them to ministerial tasks (Alfieri, 1992).

Individuals struggling with these issues can turn to their local P & A system offices for state law expertise. In 33 states, state bar associations with committees or sections on disability issues may be able to provide some preliminary information and referral assistance.[3] Concerned citizens should also make use of the resources listed below or consider contacting law school clinical programs that specialize in disability law or other experts for advice when questions arise regarding capacity to be represented. Unless persons with disabilities can be represented and can obtain redress through the legal system, inequalities in the law and society will be more difficult to challenge.

---

[3] As of May 1995, the ABA Commission on Mental and Physical Disability Law identified 33 states with disability-related entities: Alabama, Arizona, Arkansas, California, Colorado, Connecticut, Florida, Illinois, Indiana, Iowa, Kansas, Kentucky, Louisiana, Maine, Maryland, Michigan, Minnesota, Mississippi, Missouri, Montana, Nebraska, New Hampshire, New Mexico, New York, Ohio, Oklahoma, Oregon, Pennsylvania, Rhode Island, Texas, Vermont, West Virginia, and Wyoming.

Resources and Bibliography

Brakel, S. J., Parry, J. M. & Weiner, B.A. (1985). *The mentally disabled and the law*. Chicago: American Bar Foundation.

Herr, S. (1983). *Rights and advocacy for retarded people*. Lexington, MA: D. C. Heath.

Kopelman, L., & Moskop, J. C. (Eds.). (1984). *Ethics and mental retardation*. Dordrecht, Netherlands: D. Reidel.

National Association for Protection and Advocacy Systems (NAPAS) is a clearinghouse for information about the protection and advocacy systems in the 50 states and territories. (For referrals to a P & A system in your state or to P & A attorneys conversant with issues of consent to be represented, contact NAPAS at 900 Second St. NE, Suite 211, Washington, DC 20002; telephone (202) 408-9514.)

Parry, J. (1995). *Mental disability law: A primer*. Washington, DC: American Bar Association Commission on Mental and Physical Disability Law. (The ABA Commission also publishes the bimonthly *Mental and Physical Disability Law Reporter*, which contains up-to-date summaries of cases and laws with categories indexed to include the role of attorneys and advocates, individual rights, and developmental disabilities. The Commission's phone number is (202) 662-1570.)

Rozovsky, F. A. (1989 & 1996 Supp.). *Consent to treatment: A practical guide* (2nd ed.). Boston: Little, Brown.

Tremblay, P. R. (1987). On persuasion and paternalism: Lawyer decisionmaking and the questionably competent client. *Utah Law Review*, 515–584.

Ward, A. D. (1990). *The power to act: The development of Scots law for mentally handicapped people*. Glasgow: Scottish Society for the Mentally Handicapped

Westman, J. C. (Ed.). (1991). *Who speaks for the children?: The handbook of individual and class child advocacy*. Sarasota, FL: Professional Resources Exchange.

References

Alabama Disabilities Advocacy Program v. Tarwater Developmental Center, 894 F. Supp. 424 (M.D. Ala. 1995).

Alfieri, A. (1992). Disabled clients, disabling lawyers. *Hastings Law Journal, 43,* 769–851.

Alisberg, N. B. (1983). Note—Disability law—The Developmentally Disabled Assistance and Bill of Rights Act is alive and well and living in New Hampshire—Developmental Disabilities Advocacy Center, Inc. v. Melton, 689 F.2d 281 (1st Cir. 1982). *Western New England Law Review, 5,* 537–563.

American Bar Association. (1982). *Model code of professional responsibility*. Chicago: Author.

American Bar Association. (1989). Guardianship: An agenda for reform: Recommendations of the National Guardianship Symposium and policy of the American Bar Association. Washington, DC: Commission on the Mentally Disabled & Commission on Legal Problems of the Elderly, ABA.

American Bar Association. (1995). *Model rules of professional conduct*. Chicago: Author.

American Bar Association. (1995, 1997 Amendment). *Model rules of professional conduct*. Chicago: Author.

American Bar Association and Bureau of National Affairs. (1994). *Lawyers' manual on professional conduct*. Chicago: Author.

Brakel, S. J., Parry, J., & Weiner, B. A. (1985). *The mentally disabled and the law* (3rd ed.). Chicago: American Bar Foundation.

Burt, R. A. (1985). Pennhurst: A parable. In R. H. Mnookin, *In the interest of children: Advocacy, law reform, and public policy* (pp. 265–363). New York: W. H. Freeman.

Cal. Welf. and Inst. Code § 5523(a) (1984) (presuming recipient of mental health services competent for purposes of receiving advocacy services unless court finds recipient incompetent to enter into agreement with an advocate and appoints guardian *ad litem* for that purpose).

Child v. Beame, 412 F. Supp. 593 (S.D.N.Y. 1976).

Davis, P. K. (1978). Note—Qualified right to refuse medical treatment may be asserted for incompetent under doctrine of substituted judgment—Superintendent of Belchertown State School v. Saikewicz, 373 Mass. 728, 370 N.E.2d 417 (1977). *Emory Law Journal, 27,* 425–460.

Developmental Disabilities Advocacy Center, Inc. v. Melton, 689 F.2d 281 (1st Cir. 1982).

Developmentally Disabled Assistance and Bill of Rights Act, 42 U.S.C. § 6042(a)(2)(B) (1995).

Dinerstein, R. (1990). Client-centered counseling: Reappraisal and refinement. *Arizona Law Review, 32,* 501–604.

Dusky v. United States, 362 U.S. 402 (1960).

Estate of C. W. Appeal of Lorrie McKinley, Guardian *Ad Litem* for C. W., 640 A.2d 427 (Pa. Super. 1994).

Exec. Order No. 12,994, 61 Fed. Reg. 13,047 (1996) (continuing the President's Committee on Mental Retardation and broadening its membership and responsibilities).

Federal Rules of Civil Procedure (1997).

Friedman, P. (1974). The mentally handicapped citizen and institutional labor. *Harvard Law Review, 87,* 567–587.

Gillers, S., & Simon, R. D. (1998). *Regulation of lawyers: Statutes and standards.* New York: Aspen Law & Business.

Gottlich, V. (1995–1996). The role of the attorney for the defendant in adult guardianship cases: An advocate's perspective. *Maryland Journal of Contemporary Legal Issues, 7,* 191–221.

Green, B. A., & Dohrn, B. (1996). Foreword: Children and the ethical practice of law. *Fordham Law Review, 64,*1281–1298.

Guardianship of Phillip B., 188 Cal. Rptr. 781 (1983).

Halderman v. Pennhurst State School and Hospital, 446 F. Supp. 1295 (E.D. Pa. 1977), *aff'd in part, rev'd and remanded in part,* 612 F.2d 84 (3d Cir. 1979) (subsequent history omitted).

Haralambie, A. M. (1996). Response to the working group on determining the best interests of the child. *Fordham Law Review, 64,* 2013–2018.

Herr, S. (1979). The new clients: Legal services for mentally retarded persons. *Stanford Law Review, 31,* 553–611.

Herr, S. (1983). *Rights and advocacy for retarded people.* Lexington, MA: D. C. Heath.

Herr, S. (1987, November 6). Sixty-three years in "moral quarantine." *The Baltimore Sun,* A23 (opinion commentary).

Herr, S. (1989–1990). Representation of clients with disabilities: Issues of ethics and control. *New York University Review of Law & Social Change, 17,* 609–650.

Herr, S. (1995). Maximizing autonomy: Reforming personal support laws in Sweden and the United States. *JASH, 20,* 213–223.

Herr, S., Arons, S., & Wallace, R. E., Jr. (1983). *Legal rights and mental health care.* Lexington, MA: D. C. Heath.

Individuals With Disabilities Education Act, 20 U.S.C. § 1415(b)(1)(B)(2) (1998).

In re M. R., 638 A.2d 1274 (N.J. 1994).

Lelsz v. Kavanagh, 710 F.2d 1040 (5th Cir. 1983) (rejecting intervention by parent association that sought to advocate a particular policy rather than vindicate a legal right).

Luban, D. (1988). *Lawyers and justice: An empirical study.* Princeton, NJ: Princeton University Press.

Margulies, P. (1994). Access, connection, and voice: A contextual approach to representing senior citizens of questionable capacity. *Fordham Law Review, 62,* 1073–1099.

Markovits, I. (1996). Children of a lesser God: GDR lawyers in post-socialist Germany. *Michigan Law Review, 94,* 2270–2308.

Maryland Disability Law Center v. Mt. Washington Pediatric Hospital, 664 A.2d 16 (Md. App. 1995).

Md. Code Ann., Est. & Trusts, § 13-705(b) (1997).

Mickenberg, N. (1979). The silent clients: Legal and ethical considerations in representing severely and profoundly retarded individuals. *Stanford Law Review, 31,* 625–635 (noting that the guardian *ad litem* is not available in nonlitigation contexts).

Miller, A., & Keys, C. (1996). Awareness, action, and collaboration: How the self-advocacy movement is empowering for persons with developmental disabilities. *Mental Retardation, 34,* 312–319.

Minow, M. (1990). *Making all the difference: Inclusion, exclusion, and American law.* Ithaca, NY: Cornell University Press.

Mississippi Protection & Advocacy System v. Cotten, 929 F.2d 1054 (5th Cir. 1991).

NYSARC v. Carey, 393 F. Supp. 715 (E.D. N.Y. 1975); 596 F.2d 27 (2nd Cir. 1979).

Pennhurst State School and Hospital v. Halderman, 465 U.S. 89 (1984) (subsequent history omitted).

People First of Tennessee v. Clover Bottom Developmental Center, No. 3:95-1227, Settlement Agreement between People First, the United States, and the State of Tennessee (M.D. Tenn. Nov. 15, 1996) (describing plaintiff organization as having members in the three institutions sued and as having as one of its purposes "to advocate and defend the rights of persons with disabilities," and naming 18 individual plaintiffs).

Pepe, S., & Lindgren, C. (1990). Working with questionably competent clients: Ethical dilemmas in lawyering—Part I. *Best Practice Notes on Delivery of Legal Assistance to Older Persons, 4,* 2–19.

Pepe, S. D., Burns, A. M., & Lindgren, C. (1991). Working with questionably competent clients: Ethical dilemmas in lawyering—Part II. *Best Practice Notes on Delivery of Legal Assistance to Older Persons, 5,* 2–18.

Peters, J. K. (1996). The roles and content of best interests in client-directed lawyering for children in child protective proceedings. *Fordham Law Review, 64,* 1505–1570.

Rein, J. E. (1994). Clients with destructive and socially harmful choices—What's an attorney to do?: Within and beyond the competency construct. *Fordham Law Review, 62*, 1101–1176.

Rhode, D. (1982). Class conflicts in class actions. *Stanford Law Review, 34*, 1183–1262.

Robinson, L. J. (1995). Guardianship proceedings for incompetents: Ethical obligations for the attorney. *New Jersey Lawyer, 170*, 36–38.

Roca, R. P. (1994). Determining decisional capacity: A medical perspective. *Fordham Law Review, 62*, 1177–1196.

Smith, L. F. (1988). Representing the elderly client and addressing the question of competence. *Journal of Contemporary Law, 14*, 61–104.

Superintendent of Belchertown State School v. Saikewicz, 370 N.E.2d 417 (Mass. 1977).

Tremblay, P. R. (1987). On persuasion and paternalism: Lawyer decisionmaking and the questionably competent client. *Utah Law Review*, 515–584.

Turnbull, H. R. III. (Ed.). (1977). *Consent handbook.* Washington, DC: American Association on Mental Deficiency.

Wald, P. M. (1976). Basic personal and civil rights. In M. Kindred et al. (Eds.), *The mentally retarded citizen and the law* (pp. 3–26). New York: The Free Press.

CHAPTER 7

Capacity and the Courts

■

Robert D. Dinerstein and Michelle Buescher
American University, Washington College of Law

T his chapter considers the rights and responsibilities of those with mental retardation and other developmental disabilities in the criminal justice system and in civil courts. Such persons may or may not be capable of standing trial, assisting in their own defense, testifying as witnesses, or acting as jurors. This chapter discusses common standards for these questions. As stated repeatedly, the law in each state differs, and readers should investigate the law in their own jurisdiction on these points.

Apprehension and Custody of People With Mental Retardation

The police may arrest and take into custody anyone suspected of a crime, including persons with mental retardation. The law assumes that adults are competent until found to be otherwise by the court. As a result, police tend to treat all suspects alike. Because arrests may occur quickly and in an atmosphere of confusion and urgency, officers may not know or recognize that a person has mental retardation until they are well into the process of an arrest.

Because persons with mental retardation are more vulnerable when taken into custody than other individuals, law enforcement and other criminal justice officials must be trained to recognize symptoms, behavior traits, and mannerisms of persons with mental retardation (Higgins, 1995, pp. 1–2). Some voluntary agencies offer training to officers in recognition and handling of persons with mental retardation. One judge recommends that police agencies establish protocols for procedures such as arrest, questioning, screening, and referral of suspects or witnesses with mental retardation. Appropriate protocols may include protective custody, referral to an appropriate facility, having a mental retardation specialist on call, or providing access to a judicial officer (Higgins, 1995, pp. 14–17).[1]

The ABA *Criminal Justice Mental Health Standards* (1986, 1989) suggest that state statutes should define situations in which police may take persons with mental retardation into custody. They propose that the apprehension of such persons be confined to those whose conduct "represents a danger to themselves or others; and, to those who appear so gravely disabled as to be unable to provide themselves with the basic necessities of life (Standard 7-2.1(a)). Standard 7-2.1(b) proposes that police who confront persons with mental disabilities should be limited strictly to transporting them to a suitable facility for examination and treatment or habilitation.

Whenever feasible and safe, police should seek a voluntary placement of suspects with mental retardation who have been taken into emergency police custody, rather than use involuntary commitment measures (Standard 7-2.3). They should also seek the assistance of friends, advocates, relatives, or service providers of the individual (Standard 7-2.3).

Confessions and Statements in Custody

The Fifth Amendment to the United States Constitution gives those accused of crimes the right to protect themselves against self-incrimination. This right means that when the police question a person in custody (roughly equivalent to arrest), they must immediately tell the suspect that the suspect has the right to an

---

[1] The American Bar Association (ABA) *Criminal Justice Mental Health Standards* (1986, 1989) also advocate that police agencies develop written procedures. See 1986 Standard 7-2.1(c): Classes of mentally ill and mentally retarded persons subject to police emergency detention; Standard 7-2.2: Development of joint policy admitting persons detained by police for mental evaluation; Standard 7-2.8: Specialized training.

attorney, including the right to an appointed attorney if the suspect is unable to afford one, and that anything the person says can be used against him or her. These statements comprise the so-called *Miranda* rights, made famous in the Supreme Court case of *Miranda v. Arizona* (1966). A person may waive his or her *Miranda* rights as long as the waiver is voluntary, knowing, and intelligent. Mental retardation may impair an individual's ability to understand these rights. The Supreme Court ruled in *Colorado v. Connelly* (1986), however, that a defendant's mental condition cannot in itself establish whether a confession was coerced or a waiver made improperly.

In evaluating whether a confession or custodial statement is valid, and therefore admissible at a trial, courts look to the totality of the circumstances (Higgins, 1995). Relevant circumstances include the individual's inability to comprehend concepts; surrounding pressures to make a statement; the suggestibility of the individual; the questioner's use of leading questions; any information that may have been supplied by the questioner, albeit inadvertently; and the individual's ability to understand consequences (Higgins; see also Luckasson, 1995).

Counsel and the court should assess the voluntariness and reliability of the statements of a person with mental retardation before such statements are admitted into evidence. A police officer's conduct that would normally not be considered coercive may compromise the voluntariness of statements given by persons with mental retardation, who may have a strong desire to please those in positions of authority. Where the court finds a significant lack of voluntariness, it should exclude the statement from evidence. If the statement truly was voluntary, however, then it should be admissible (Standard 7-5.8(b)).

Likewise, if the court finds that the reliability of a statement is doubtful because of a person's mental retardation, it should exclude the statement; where not excluded, the court should permit counsel to present evidence regarding the effect of mental retardation on the reliability of the statement (Standard 7-5.8(a)).

Forming the Attorney-Client Relationship

A criminal defense attorney has a duty to consult with the client, keep the client informed, and assist the client in making informed decisions about the case. Rules of ethics governing the legal profession prohibit the attorney from unilaterally deciding what is in the client's best interests. The criminal defendant, for example, normally must make certain fundamental decisions. These include whether to plead guilty or not guilty, whether to waive a jury trial, whether to testify, and whether to appeal (*Jones v. Barnes,* 1983, at 751; ABA, 1983, Rule 1.2). A client's mental retardation, however, may affect the "normal" lawyer-client relationship. If, for example, the client cannot process information or understand the lawyer's advice, the lawyer may be forced to assume some decision-making responsibility for the client or raise the issue of the person's competency to stand trial (Uphoff, 1988, p. 69).

Lawyers may find it difficult to respect the choices of their clients who have mental retardation, particularly if those choices seem irrational or contrary to what the lawyer would do if the lawyer were the client. The lawyer may feel pressure to assume a paternalistic role in the decision-making process, steering the client toward certain choices in order to avoid harmful consequences. Or the lawyer may feel obligated to inform the court of the lawyer's inability to follow the client's directions and may question the client's competency (Uphoff, p. 70). The decision to take this step is a difficult one, because it may be harmful to the client's interests and could compromise the lawyer's duty of loyalty to the client.

The ABA *Model Rules of Professional Conduct* (1983) state that if a client's ability to make adequately considered decisions is impaired, the lawyer "shall, as far as reasonably possible, maintain a normal lawyer-client relationship with the client" (Rule 1.14). The commentary to Rule 1.14 states: "A client lacking legal competence often retains the ability to understand, weigh options, and reach conclusions about matters affecting his well-being." Of course, there are degrees of competence; some impaired clients are capable of making some decisions but not others. "Accordingly, the lawyer is directed to treat the mentally disabled client with respect and to allow the client as much autonomy as possible" (Uphoff, 1988, p. 75). The lawyer may take "protective action" regarding a client "only when the lawyer reasonably believes that the client cannot adequately act in the client's own interest." (ABA, 1983, Rule 1.14(b)).

While attempting to treat the client with mental retardation like any other client, the defense attorney may have to make special efforts to communicate with the client. Lawyers who are inexperienced in working with persons with mental retardation may feel frustrated in their attempts to converse with them. Mental retardation professionals, family members, and advocates can educate lawyers about the best way to proceed (Bonnie, 1992, pp. 100, 114–115). Lawyers should know that some persons with mental retardation have difficulty:

- understanding directions or procedures;

- expressing their needs to others;

- understanding the consequences of making an agreement or giving consent;

- remembering;

- exercising judgment;

- making decisions;

- understanding rapid speech, complex sentences, and abstract concepts; and

- reading and writing (Parry, 1995, p. 7).

In addition, lawyers should be aware that many times persons with mental retardation are eager to please others and seek their approval. They can be especially eager to please those who are in positions of authority, sometimes taking the blame or making statements that are not in their own interest. Some persons with mental retardation may also:

- communicate through mimicking;

- bluff understanding; or

- communicate by smiling inappropriately (Hawkins, 1995, pp. 1, 4–6).

Lawyers should be aware of these differences so they can communicate effectively with and understand the wishes of their clients.

Raising the Issue of Competency

A person with mental retardation is presumed to be competent until a court determines otherwise. But when the court, defense counsel, or prosecutor has a bona fide doubt about a defendant's competence, they are obligated to raise the question of competency (*Pate v. Robinson,* 1966). Because an incompetent defendant cannot waive incompetency as a defense, it is a violation of due process to permit the person to be tried (ABA, 1986, 1989, Standard 7-4.2, commentary, p. 180). Due process requires a competency hearing, and courts have recommended that, in order to determine whether competency is questionable, "evidence of a defendant's irrational behavior, his demeanor at trial, and any prior medical opinion" should be considered (*Drope v. Missouri,* 1975, at 180).

Attorneys representing questionably competent persons face a difficult decision when informing the court of the client's possible incompetency is contrary to the client's wishes or best interests. To act contrary to the client's wishes is potentially to breach the ethical obligations of confidentiality, zealousness, avoidance of conflict of interest, and loyalty to the client (see Cohen, 1998, p. 557). As a result, some defense attorneys are reluctant to raise competency if they believe that doing so will be harmful to the client. For example, if the attorney raises the issue of incompetency, and the court finds the client incompetent, the client may be committed to a mental institution for a lengthy period. One commentator analyzes the competing pressures as follows:

> The lawyer may feel bound...to raise competency to protect the client's right to make fundamental decisions even though raising the issue is detrimental to the client. Counsel may also be uncomfortable withholding

information from the court about the client's impaired mental condition. Aware of her role as an officer of the court and concerned about not misleading the court, counsel may seriously question the propriety of allowing her marginally competent client to act, such as pleading guilty, when the competency issue remains unresolved (Uphoff, 1988, p. 74).

The ABA *Model Rules of Professional Conduct* (1983) recognize such a dilemma, but do not resolve it. The comment to Rule 1.14 states: "The lawyer's position in such cases is an unavoidably difficult one." The comment suggests that the lawyer "may seek guidance from an appropriate diagnostician." The ABA *Criminal Justice Mental Health Standards* (1986, 1989) recommend that, if the defense counsel doubts a client's competence in good faith, the attorney should move for the evaluation of the defendant's competence to stand trial, even if the client objects to such a motion being made (Standard 7-4.2(c)). An authoritative text suggests that the defense counsel weigh the following factors in deciding whether to raise the competency issue: careful analysis of the degree of the client's mental impairment, the importance of the decision being considered, the type of case, and the costs and benefits to the client of alternative courses of action (Amsterdam, 1988, pp. 314–318).

Defense counsel should always discuss the competency issue with the client and try to elicit the client's response. If the client can articulate a choice, and it is reasoned and plausible, the client should be permitted to waive a defense of incompetency just as individuals without mental retardation are allowed to waive other rights. The following questions may be helpful to the defense counsel in reaching a decision on the competency issue:

1. Does the client understand the roles of the major participants in the adversary process?

2. Does the client appreciate defense counsel's function, and is he capable of trusting and working with counsel?

3. Does the client recognize the difference between a guilty plea and a trial?

4. Is the client aware of the nature of the charges he faces, the seriousness of such charges, and the possible consequences?

5. Is the client capable of discussing the factual basis of the charges, possible defenses, and problems with accounts given by prosecution witnesses?

6. Can the client testify in a relevant, coherent manner?

7. Is the client able to discuss likely outcomes and make choices regarding plea options or defense strategy?

8. Can the client control his motor and verbal behavior to the extent that court proceedings will not be disrupted? (Uphoff, 1988, p. 99).

After fully discussing the matter with the client and balancing the costs and benefits to the client, defense counsel must decide whether or not to raise the competency issue. If the defense counsel decides not to do so, counsel should carefully document the decision–making process. Several appellate courts have held that a lawyer's failure to raise the issue of competency could constitute a deprivation of the defendant's right to effective assistance of counsel (see, e.g., *Speedy v. Wyrick*, 1983; *Owsley v. Peyton,*1966; but see *Enriquez v. Procunier,* 1984, 1985). Uphoff, 1988, p. 93, proposes that to allay their concern that defense counsel not manufacture reasons after the fact to explain their failure to raise a competency issue, courts could require counsel to file a sealed memorandum with the trial judge explaining why no competence issue was raised.

If the attorney does choose to raise the issue of competency, a motion for a competency hearing may be made "at any time after the commencement of a prosecution for an offense and prior to the sentencing of the defendant" (Insanity Defense Reform Act of 1984, 18 U.S.C. § 4241(a), 1998; this statute governs only federal proceedings).

Competency Evaluations

When the issue of defendant's competency is raised, the court will order a competency evaluation. The court may order this evaluation without the defendant's consent (*United States v. Huguenin*, 1991; see also *United States v. Watson*, 1993, at 734). In the federal courts, the court may be required to provide the defendant with a psychiatric expert for the competency hearing. (According to 18 U.S.C. § 3006A(e)(1), 1997 Supp., an indigent defendant is entitled to "investigative, expert, or other services necessary for adequate representation"; see also Herseth, 1996, p. 1066; cf. *Ake v. Oklahoma*, 1985.) In state courts, while the defendant does not have the right to have counsel present at the examination, the defendant does have a Sixth Amendment constitutional right to consult with counsel before submitting to a court–ordered psychiatric examination (Herseth, p. 1068). The Supreme Court, in *Buchanan v. Kentucky* (1987, at 424–25), stated that the defendant's Sixth Amendment right to consultation is fulfilled so long as counsel is "informed about the scope and nature of the proceeding" and is aware of "the possible uses to which petitioner's statements in the proceedings could be put."

The state may not use a defendant's statements made in a competency evaluation against him at trial nor at a subsequent sentencing hearing unless the defendant, prior to the evaluation, has knowingly waived his or her Fifth Amendment right against self-incrimination (*Estelle v. Smith*, 1981, at 462–463, 469). This rule is limited to situations "where the defendant did not initiate the psychiatric examination or attempt to introduce psychiatric evidence at trial" (*Buchanan v. Kentucky*, 1987, cited in Herseth, 1996, p. 1073). In 1987, the Supreme Court stated that a defendant's Fifth Amendment rights are not violated when the testimony of the psychiatrist is limited to the question of the competency of defendant (*Buchanan v. Kentucky*, at 424–425).

A thorough and complete evaluation of competency to stand trial should include the following:

- a review of school records;
- a review of previous evaluations;
- appropriate intelligence testing;
- appropriate achievement testing;
- an interview with the defendant;

- an interview with people who know the defendant; and

- an observation of interactions between the defendant and lawyer (Luckasson, 1995).

In addition, evaluators should be required to inform the defendant of the purpose and nature of the evaluation, the potential uses to which disclosures may be put, the conditions under which the prosecutor will have access to information and reports based on the evaluation, and the consequences of a refusal to cooperate (ABA, 1986, 1989, Standard 7-3.5(b); see also George, 1985, p. 353).

Tests for Competency

A defendant is generally found competent to stand trial if the defendant can understand the charges lodged against him, the criminal process, and the potential punishments and can assist in his own defense (Luckasson, 1995). Most states have adopted the test set forth by the Supreme Court in *Dusky v. United States* (1960, at 402), which requires the court to decide whether a defendant has "sufficient present ability to consult with his lawyer with a reasonable degree of rational understanding and whether he has a rational as well as factual understanding of the proceedings against him." In 1993, the Supreme Court ruled that the tests for competency to waive counsel and to plead guilty are the same as that for competency to stand trial. States may supplement the competency standards set forth in *Dusky* but are not constitutionally required to do so (*Godinez v. Moran*, at 398, 402).

According to federal law, the court must find that a defendant is incompetent to stand trial by a preponderance of the evidence (Insanity Defense Reform Act of 1984, 18 U.S.C. § 4241(d), 1998). The federal statute, however, does not allocate the burden of proof, and the circuit courts are split as to whether the defense or prosecution bears the burden of proving defendant's competency (Herseth, 1996, p. 1072). The Supreme Court has held that, while it is not unconstitutional to place the burden on the defendant to prove his incompetency to stand trial, that burden may not be greater than a preponderance of the evidence (*Medina v. California*, 1992; *Cooper v. Oklahoma*, 1996).

Capacity to Serve as a Witness

"Every person is competent to be a witness," according to Federal Rules of Evidence Rule 601, unless provided otherwise in the Rules. A witness must possess "personal knowledge of a particular fact" and be "capable of declaring by oath or affirmation to tell the truth" in order to testify. In deciding whether a person with mental retardation should testify, the ultimate question is whether the witness is so lacking in ability to observe, recall, or narrate testimony as to be untrustworthy. The question has also been framed as "whether the witness has the ability to tell the truth, and to perceive, recall, and tell about events in question." In addition, neither the adjudication of mental incompetence nor the fact that the witness has spent time in a mental institution precludes the witness from testifying (Graham, 1983, p. 37).

Mental capacity can affect both the weight and admissibility of testimony. If a witness is so severely limited that a reasonable juror could not believe the witness's testimony, the court must find the witness incompetent to testify. The court may conduct a preliminary hearing and a forensic examination of the person to assist in its determination (Graham, pp. 42–43). Questions that should be addressed during this examination include:

- Can the person tell the difference between true and false statements?

- Does the person understand the obligation to tell the truth?

- How does the person's general intellectual ability relate to perceptions of the event?

- How good is the person's memory and ability to communicate?

- If the witness cannot perform the above functions completely, which, if any, of the functions can the person perform partially?

- What accommodations might help the person participate as a witness? (Luckasson, 1995, pp. 14–15).

Incompetence in another area (e.g., incompetency to stand trial or to waive counsel) does not necessarily mean that person is incompetent to be a witness (Luckasson, p. 13).

In criminal cases, prosecutors focus greatly on the credibility of the state's witnesses, including most particularly the credibility of the complaining witness or victim. When that complaining witness is a person with mental retardation, prosecutors may have a tendency to drop (or greatly reduce) charges against a defendant because of their view that a jury would not believe the person's testimony. Advocates and mental retardation professionals can work with prosecutor's offices to sensitize them to the mental capacities of witnesses with mental retardation, allowing at a minimum for more finely tuned assessments of credibility and competency. In some instances, a prosecutor may be able to persuade a court to permit the witness with mental retardation to testify in chambers or on videotape, though a defendant's Sixth Amendment right to confront the witnesses against him or her may limit such substitutes for direct testimony.

Capacity to Serve as a Juror

The question may arise as to whether a person with mental retardation or other developmental disability is competent to serve as a juror in a civil or criminal case. According to Section 504 of the Rehabilitation Act of 1973, "a trial court's determination of juror competency must be based on an individual's ability to evaluate the evidence in a particular case" (29 U.S.C. § 794, 1998). To deliberate satisfactorily, jurors must be able to understand the issues at trial and be able to make a fair judgment of the merits (Bleyer, McCarty, & Wood, 1994). Considerations that may affect a person's ability to serve on a jury include:

- the inability to maintain concentration over time;

- difficulty in maintaining stamina during long waiting periods;

- inability to screen out external stimuli;

- difficulty in managing time pressures and deadlines;

- difficulty in becoming oriented in unfamiliar surroundings;

- difficulty in making decisions under time pressure or stress;

- being affected by psychotropic medications; and

- inability to function in uncomfortable temperatures and humidity levels (Bleyer, McCarty, & Wood, p. 18).

An attorney examining a questionably competent juror should explore the person's ability to receive and evaluate particular evidence that will be presented in the case. In preparation for this task, known as *voir dire*, counsel should review the list of communication difficulties described above.

Thirty-eight states exclude people who are incompetent "by reason of physical or mental ability to render satisfactory jury services." Thirty-nine states also exclude jurors who are unable to read, speak, or understand the English language; 12 states prohibit jury service by persons of unsound mind or who are insane or adjudicated incompetent. The vagueness of these categories leaves a great deal of room for judicial interpretation (Bleyer, McCarty, & Wood, p. 9). Since the passage of Section 504 of the Rehabilitation Act and the Americans With Disabilities Act, courts have, however, overturned the categorical exclusion of certain categories of persons with disabilities (such as people who are blind) as an irrational interference with a basic right of citizenship (*Galloway v. Superior Court of the District of Columbia*, 1993, at 20).

Conclusion

The law requires that reasonable accommodation be given to those with disabilities. This requirement includes the criminal and civil courts. Every effort should be made to treat those with disabilities as any other person charged with a crime, appearing as a witness in any proceeding, or serving as a juror. However, when the person's disabilities are too limiting, the court and those working in the system may have to decide how to best protect the person and his or her constitutional rights. The criminal justice system and its trial counsel have long familiarity with these balancing issues; the civil justice system is still working out the appropriate accommodations. Both systems must avoid "the tendency on the part of officialdom to overgeneralize about [people with disabilities]" and must challenge "archaic stereotypes thrust upon [people with disabilities]" (*Galloway v. Superior Court of the District of Columbia,* 1993, at 16–17). Courts and lawyers, no less than other professionals, need—and have sometimes sought (e.g., *In re M. R.,* 1994, at 1286)—training to better communicate with, and thus enhance the capacity of, persons with mental retardation who participate in the court system (cf. Ellis & Luckasson, 1985).

References

Ake v. Oklahoma, 470 U.S. 68 (1985) (state is required to provide indigent defendant with assistance of psychiatrist where defendant has made preliminary showing that sanity at time of offense is likely to be significant factor at trial).

American Bar Association. (1983). *Model rules of professional conduct.* Chicago: Author.

American Bar Association. (1986, 1989). *The ABA criminal justice mental health standards.* Chicago: Author. (These standards, adopted in 1983 and 1984 and amended in 1987 and 1988, represent official American Bar Association policy on matters relating to people with mental disabilities and the criminal justice system.)

Amsterdam, A. G. (1988). Trial manual for the defense of criminal cases (5th ed., Vol. 1). Philadelphia: American Law Institute.

Bleyer, K., McCarty, K. S., & Wood, E. (1994). *Into the jury box: A disability accommodation guide for state courts.* Washington, DC: American Bar Association.

Bonnie, R. J. (1992). The competency of defendants with mental retardation to assist in their own defense. In R. W. Conley, R. Luckasson, & G. N. Bouthilet (Eds.), *The criminal justice system and mental retardation: Defendants and victims.* Baltimore: Paul H. Brookes.

Buchanan v. Kentucky, 483 U.S. 402 (1987).

Cohen, J. A. (1998). The attorney-client privilege, ethical rules, and the impaired criminal defendant. *University of Miami Law Review 52,* 529 (citations omitted).

Colorado v. Connelly, 479 U.S. 157 (1986).

Cooper v. Oklahoma, 517 U.S. 348 (1996).

Drope v. Missouri, 420 U.S. 162 (1975) (holding that the trial court has a duty to investigate intimations of defendant's procedural incompetence).

Dusky v. United States, 362 U.S. 402 (1960).

Ellis, J. W. & Luckasson, R. A. (1985). Mentally retarded criminal defendants. *George Washington Law Review, 53,* 414 (for a helpful discussion of many of the issues facing defendants with mental retardation).

Enriquez v. Procunier, 752 F.2d 111 (5th Cir. 1984), *cert. denied* 471 U.S. 1126 (1985) (holding that defense counsel could, for tactical reasons, decide not to raise the competency issue).

Estelle v. Smith, 451 U.S. 454 (1981).

Federal Rules of Evidence, Rule 601 (1997).

Galloway v. Superior Court of the District of Columbia, 816 F. Supp. 12 (D.D.C. 1993) (enjoining court system from categorically excluding persons who are blind from jury service).

George, B. J., Jr. (1985). Symposium on the ABA Criminal Justice Mental Health Standards: An overview. *George Washington Law Review, 53,* 338.

Godinez v. Moran, 509 U.S. 389 (1993).

Graham, M. H. (1983). *Evidence text, rules, illustrations, and problems,* 37, 42. St. Paul, MN: The National Institute for Trial Advocacy.

Hawkins, S. (1995). Communicating with the mentally retarded. In R. Luckasson & E. E. Vance (Eds.), *Defendants, victims, and witnesses with mental retardation: An instructional guide for judges and judicial educators.* Reno, NV: National Judicial College.

Herseth, S. M. (1996). Competency to stand trial. In twenty-fifth annual review of criminal procedure. *Georgetown Law Journal, 84,* 641.

Higgins, N. (1995). Courtroom accommodation of defendants, victims, and witnesses with mental retardation. In R. Luckasson & E. E. Vance (Eds.), *Defendants, victims, and witnesses with mental retardation: An instructional guide for judges and judicial educators.* Reno, NV: National Judicial College.

In re M. R., 638 A.2d 1274 (N.J. 1994).

Insanity Defense and Reform Act of 1984, 18 U.S.C. § 4241(a),(d) (1998).

Jones v. Barnes, 463 U.S. 745 (1983).

Luckasson, R. (1995). Identification of defendants, victims, and witnesses with mental retardation. In R. Luckasson & E. E. Vance (Eds.), *Defendants, victims, and witnesses with mental retardation: An instructional guide for judges and judicial educators.* Reno, NV: National Judicial College.

Medina v. California, 505 U.S. 437 (1992).

Miranda v. Arizona, 384 U.S. 436 (1966).

Owsley v. Peyton, 368 F.2d 1002 (4th Cir. 1966).

Parry. J. (1995). *Mental disability law: A primer* (5th ed.). Washington, DC: American Bar Association Commission on Mental and Physical Disability Law.

Pate v. Robinson, 383 U.S. 375 (1966).

Rehabilitation Act of 1973, 29 U.S.C. § 794 (1998).

Speedy v. Wyrick, 702 F. 2d 723 (8th Cir. 1983).

Uphoff, R. J. (1988). The role of the criminal defense lawyer in representing the mentally impaired defendant: Zealous advocate or officer of the court? *Wisconsin Law Review, 65,* 69.

18 U.S.C. § 3006A(e)(1) (1997 Supp.).

United States v. Huguenin, 950 F.2d 23 (1st Cir. 1991).

United States v. Watson, 1 F.3d 733 (8th Cir. 1993) (noting that the trial court did not violate defendant's rights by ordering competency examination on defense counsel's motion when defendant refused to assist counsel and failed to appear for trial).

CHAPTER 8

Consent to Extraordinary Interventions

■

Stanley S. Herr
University of Maryland School of Law

Joan L. O'Sullivan
University of Maryland School of Law

Robert D. Dinerstein
American University, Washington College of Law

C ertain procedures or interventions carry such risks or impinge on human dignity to such an extent that society imposes extra safeguards on the consent-giving process. Although there is considerable controversy over which procedures deserve higher levels of scrutiny and legal protection, this chapter identifies several areas that historically have been subjected to close regulation. These areas are not intended to be inclusive of all possible extraordinary or hazardous interventions. The topics briefly discussed below are (a) participation in research trials, (b) consent to be the subject of aversive therapy, (c) sterilization, (d) termination of parental rights, and (e) consent to admission to facilities for people with mental retardation or other developmental disabilities.

Consent to Participate in Research Trials

The use of human subjects in biomedical research poses real dilemmas for those with developmental disabilities. (For a discussion of the related topics of Human Experimentation and Behavioral and Social Research, see Turnbull, 1977, pp. 56–63.) In the past, research has been performed on persons with disabilities without their knowledge or consent, or the consent of any surrogate. One of the most egregious examples occurred at the Willowbrook State Hospital, where some institutional residents were deliberately infected with viral hepatitis and later contracted the illness (see Brakel, Parry, & Weiner, 1985, p. 288 n.475). Such abuses resulted in federal regulations (45 C.F.R. Part 46, Protection of Human Subjects) and state regulations (e.g., New York's statute[1]), and court cases (e.g., *Wyatt v. Stickney,* 1972, at 401–402; *NYSARC v. Carey,* 1975) regulating human-subject research studies. These regulations have protected persons with disabilities to some extent.

However, as recently as 1996, a court found abuse of mentally impaired subjects in medical research. A New York court brought several research studies to a sudden halt when it found that state regulations did not adequately protect persons with disabilities (*T. D v. New York State Office of Mental Health,* 1996). The plaintiffs in that case challenged research being done on patients in state-licensed facilities. In many cases, the patients were not able to consent to participate in the studies, and surrogates had given consent instead. Some of the research involved trials of psychotropic and antipsychotic drugs that had long-lasting or potentially fatal side effects. Other trials involved painful testing procedures. There was no expectation that the research subjects would directly benefit from participating in the studies. The court found that the use of subjects unable to give informed consent violated their constitutional rights to due process and personal autonomy. It held that the state regulations did not balance properly the state's interest in diagnosing and treating mental disabilities with the rights of patients in its facilities.

---

[1] New York's statute, Public Health Law Article 24-A § 2440: "Safeguarding the rights and welfare of individual human subjects in the conduct of…human research projects is a matter of vital state concern. Every human being has the right to be protected against the possible conduct of medical or psychological research upon his [or her] body without his [or her] voluntary informed consent.…Accordingly, it shall be the policy of this state to protect its people against the unnecessary and improper risk of pain, suffering or injury resulting from human research conducted without their knowledge or consent."

Achieving the proper balance between advancing research that will benefit humanity and protecting the rights of persons with disabilities is extremely difficult. The goals of medical researchers are laudable—to find a cure for a particular disability—but potential conflicts of interest also exist. Researchers may be under pressure to advance their own academic careers or to produce research results for drug companies funding their projects.

In addition, vulnerable people may feel undue pressure to join a study. They may be reluctant to refuse to participate, because they fear angering or disappointing those who treat them. Residents of institutions are particularly susceptible to pressure to go along with a study, for their day-to-day care may depend on those encouraging them to participate. Residents of institutions are a convenient population on which to conduct studies because they are more easily observed and controlled than individuals living on their own.

Researchers may seek to avoid applying undue pressure on persons with disabilities by obtaining consent from surrogates. However, when surrogates consent to a person's participation, they may not have that person's wishes or best interests in mind. One study showed that 31% of surrogates consented to the subject's participation even though they believed that the subject would refuse to join the study. Further, 20% of the proxies agreed to allow the subject to participate, even though they themselves would have refused (Warren et al., 1986).

Advocates for those with disabilities should be alert to potential abuses connected with research studies. If other subjects are available, research on vulnerable persons should be avoided. Research on people with disabilities may be more justifiable if it concerns the ailment or condition that causes the vulnerability; there is a chance the research will directly benefit the person; the research presents a low level of risk to the person; or the project has been approved by advocates for people with disabilities who have no conflict of interest (Lo, 1995, p. 256). In any case, researchers and their sponsoring institutions must obtain the person's valid informed consent before conducting any research on a person with disabilities (see generally Brakel, Parry, &

Weiner, 1985, pp. 228–294). Those people interested in this issue also should consult the extensive recent work in Maryland (Office of Maryland Attorney Gen., 1998; Symposium, 1998) and at the federal level (National Bioethics Advisory Commission, 1998) regarding the contours of permissible research on people with mental disorders.

Aversive Interventions

The use of aversive therapy to control or change self-destructive or violent behavior in people with developmental disabilities is the subject of heated debate (Turnbull, 1977, p. 52–55). Aversive therapy includes a wide range of techniques, from verbal reprimands to the use of electric shocks and noxious or painful stimuli (Harris & Handleman, 1990, pp. 2–3). Some professionals in the field, families, and other advocates for people with developmental disabilities have called for a strict ban on its use. Others claim that it can be effective as a last resort for extreme behavior (Favell, 1990, p. 47).

The effectiveness of aversive therapy is far from proven, and research on its use proceeds. However, the mildest use of aversive therapy (other than verbal reprimands) is subject to the same requirements of informed consent as other medical treatments. The most extreme forms of it, without proper consent, may open the professional to criminal charges for assault and battery or civil actions for negligence or breach of contract.

There should be valid informed consent for any program of behavior modification. If the person is an adult and able to consent, staff should obtain that person's direct consent. If the person is a minor or an adult who cannot consent because of lack of capacity, staff should seek appropriate authorization from a surrogate or court-appointed guardian applying a "substituted judgment" standard of consent.

There should be heightened scrutiny for the use of aversive therapy. Court intervention should precede use of the more intrusive and punitive focus of aversive therapy. The court should be informed about the precise nature of the proposed treatment and should determine that the treatment is the least restrictive available; is in conformity with state law; and does not constitute a deprivation of the person's civil rights (*Guardianship of Weedon*, 1991).

Aversive therapy remains a legal, ethical, and moral quagmire for the professional treating those with developmental disabilities. Obtaining informed consent for this procedure is only one of several major obstacles to its use.

Sterilization

Partly in response to the abuses of the era of eugenic sterilization and beyond (Trent, 1994, pp. 184–224), sterilization of persons with mental retardation is frequently the subject of detailed state statutes. The now discredited 1927 U.S. Supreme Court case of *Buck v. Bell* had upheld a Virginia statute permitting involuntary sterilization. In the ensuing decades, more and more states have stricken involuntary sterilization from the statute books.[2] Even after some statutes had been declared unconstitutional, the practice had continued, particularly as a condition to being discharged from an institution. Thus, in the landmark right-to-habilitation case of *Wyatt v. Aderholt* (1974), the federal district court held that such a procedure could be performed only where there was a "full panoply of constitutional protections" accorded to the person. Those procedures included notice, expert evaluation, a special review committee documenting the director's decision, personal interview with the person, the appointment of legal counsel for the person, a finding by the committee that sterilization was appropriate and necessary beyond any doubt, and the opportunity for further review by a human rights committee.

A long string of common law cases has enumerated rigorous substantive and procedural standards that must be met before someone can be sterilized without her direct and fully informed

---

[2] But at least one state has not banned eugenic sterilization. At least as of 1995, North Carolina still had a statute that permitted directors of state institutions to petition a court for sterilization of a person with mental retardation when deemed to be for the "public good" or to prevent such person from having a child that "would have a tendency to serious physical, mental or nervous disease" (N.C. Gen. Stat. §§ 35-39(2), (3), 1995, cited in Zumpano-Canto, 1996, pp. 84-86 & nn.18-19).

consent. Typical of those cases is *Wentzel v. Montgomery General Hospital* (1982). There, Maryland's highest court required clear and convincing evidence that there was no less drastic alternative, the proposed operation was in the individual's best interests, and the operation was required as a matter of medical necessity. Although a handful of cases has authorized such operations where these type of evidentiary burdens could be met, many of the reported cases have denied permission to sterilize persons with mental retardation who are not competent to make that decision for themselves.

A recent exception to this trend, perhaps, is *Wirsig v. Michigan Protection and Advocacy Services* (1998), in which the Michigan Supreme Court upheld a probate court's decision to permit the mother (and guardian) of a woman with mental retardation to consent to her daughter's sterilization. The Michigan Protection and Advocacy office had persuaded an intermediate appellate court that the guardian did not have the authority under state law to consent to the procedure for her ward. In reversing the intermediate court, the Michigan Supreme Court concluded that the ward should not be denied the option of sterilization solely because she was incompetent to decide whether to become pregnant. The court concluded the guardian should be permitted to make a substituted judgment decision about sterilization on behalf of her ward.

Wirsig suggests that, with appropriate safeguards, courts may approve requests for sterilization on behalf of people with mental retardation to the extent these requests can be characterized as requests for medical care otherwise available to people in the community. A similar spirit underlies *Estate of C. W.* (1994), where the court upheld a probate court's approval of the request of a mother (and guardian) for sterilization of her daughter, over the objection of the guardian *ad litem* who represented the position of opposition to the procedure. To the extent the person for whom sterilization is sought is living in a noncoercive setting and has a close relationship with the petitioner, courts may be more inclined to grant petitions for sterilization. But even in these cases, there is substantial value in a court appointing a guardian *ad litem* whose principal job is to raise possible objections to the procedure, so as to assure that all arguments, pro and con, are heard. Moreover, if the sterilization is performed on a person with mental retardation based on that person's ability to give direct consent, officials who perform such sterilizations must be sure that the person is capable of giving informed consent. Otherwise, these officials face potential liability under 42 U.S.C. §§ 1983 & 1985(3) (see *Lake v. Arnold*, 1997).

Consent and Termination of Parental Rights

Although consent to parenting is not an issue, a person's fitness or capacity to retain child-rearing responsibilities can be a problem. When termination of parental rights is threatened, parents may face decisions as to whether to consent to parenting assistance, such as parent training, homemaker services, therapy, and intergenerational support. The ability to consent and cooperate with social service workers is especially important in this high-risk area.

Parental rights, including most basically the right to be a parent, are fundamental constitutional rights, no less for parents with mental retardation than for parents of typical intelligence (*Stanley v. Illinois*, 1972; see Impact, 1998). The state may seek to terminate parental rights, however, when it can demonstrate by clear and convincing evidence that it is in the best interests of the child to do so (Areen, 1992).

Mental disabilities, including mental retardation, do not per se prevent a person from exercising his or her legal role as a parent (*In re A. M. S.*, 1988; see Watkins, 1995). But if, as a result of a parent's mental retardation and facts or omissions, a court deems a person unable or unwilling to be an adequate parent, the person can involuntarily lose parental rights.

Parents with mental retardation have sought to use the Americans With Disabilities Act (ADA) of 1990 to defend their parental rights. Under Title II of the ADA (42 U.S.C. § 12132), no qualified individual with a disability may be excluded from the benefits of the "services, programs, or activities" of a state or local government on the basis of disability. A threshold question is whether termination of parental rights is a "service, program, or activity" of a state or local government. A number of courts have concluded that termination proceedings are not "services, programs, or activities" and, as such, do not come within the reach of Title II (e.g., *In re B. S.,* 1997). Section 504 of the Rehabilitation Act (29 U.S.C § 794, 1998), which is essentially coextensive with Title II, also has been held not to reach termination proceedings (e.g., *New Mexico v. Penny J.,* 1994).

A more fruitful approach to challenge termination proceedings is to examine the extent to which parents with mental retardation have consented to necessary social and rehabilitative services, including assistance in parenting. Not all states require the provision of such services, but where they do, the parent with mental retardation may be able to forestall termination proceedings by demonstrating that a reasonable accommodation of a disability would be the offer of parenting services (e.g., *In re C. M.,* 1994, concluding, however, that services provided were adequate; *In re Welfare of A. J. R.,* 1995). Parents with mental retardation and advocates must identify specific necessary services in order to prevail. One court has written that, had its state statutes required the provision of reasonable services prior to termination, the ADA would have applied (*Stone v. Daviess County Division of Children and Family Services,*1995). Even when a court holds that the ADA may not be used as a defense in a termination proceeding, it may be possible for the parent to bring a separate action under the ADA claiming discrimination on the basis of disability (e.g., *In re Torrance P.,* 1994).

Whereas a social service agency may be required to offer reasonable services, the parent with mental retardation may choose to refuse them, in which case the failure to provide services would not violate the ADA (e.g., *In re Caresse B.,* 1997).

Termination of parental rights cases primarily raise issues of state law, and persons with mental retardation and their advocates need to consult their jurisdiction's statutes and regulations to determine the full range of rights a parent with mental retardation possesses. Some state courts have required appointment of an attorney for a parent facing termination of parental rights (*In re Lindsey C.,* 1995). Other courts have required the social service agency to continue to provide educational or other services

designed to render unnecessary termination of parental rights
(e.g., *In re Elizabeth R.,* 1995).

Admissions to Facilities and Programs[3]

A general discussion of voluntary and involuntary commitment to
state facilities for people with mental retardation and developmental disabilities is beyond the scope of this book. Indeed, it is
increasingly rare for people with mental retardation to be committed (whether voluntarily or involuntarily) to congregate state
institutions. Nevertheless, "voluntary" commitments raise a special consent issue worth noting. (Because commitments of
people with mental retardation to state institutions were often
sought by parents who may well not have had alternatives, a
number of courts have construed "voluntary" commitments
essentially to be involuntary, such that it would be appropriate to
analyze institutional conditions as arising from state deprivations
of liberty; e.g., *Halderman v. Pennhurst State School & Hospital,*
1977, at 1310 & n.46; *Wyatt v. Stickney,* 1972, at 390 n.5 (presumption that all residents of Partlow were involuntarily there).)

In *Zinermon v. Burch* (1990), the Supreme Court held that a
person with mental illness stated a claim for violation of his
federal civil rights when he was admitted as a voluntary patient
to a state mental institution under circumstances where the
admitting personnel knew or should have known that he was
unable to give informed consent to his voluntary admission. The
same principles should apply in cases in which a person with
mental retardation seeks voluntary admission, or, more likely,
where a parent or other relative seeks the person's admission. In
In re Hop (1981), the California Supreme Court held that the
"voluntary" admission of a woman with a developmental disability sought by her mother to a state hospital violated due process
when she received neither a judicial hearing nor was able to
make a knowing and intelligent request for admission.

As with other questions of consent discussed in this book, the
level of formality required for determining consent will vary in

---

[3] See generally Turnbull, 1977, pp. 39-47. Note that the holding in the *Bartley* case, referred to at
pp. 46-47, was later superseded in *Parham v. J. R.* (1979).

light of the restriction on liberty necessitated by admission to the program or facility (Winick, 1994). The strongest case for requiring formal consent, either from the person with mental retardation or a surrogate decision maker, is where commitment to a large, congregate facility is sought.

Conclusion

Professionals in the field must be especially sensitive to obtaining consent to experimental, hazardous, and/or irreversible procedures. Counsel should be consulted to gain a detailed understanding of the law in a particular state. Such caution is appropriate given the legal liabilities and fundamental human rights implicated. The law is also in flux in many of these areas and judges are mindful of avoiding the human rights abuses of the past, when standards were less protective of the person's interests.

References

Americans With Disabilities Act, Title II, 42 U.S.C. § 12132 (1998).

Areen, J. (1992). *Cases and materials on family law* (3rd ed.). Westbury, NY: Foundation Press.

Brakel, S. J., Parry, J., & Weiner, B. A. (1985). *The mentally disabled and the law* (3rd ed.). Chicago: American Bar Foundation.

Buck v. Bell, 274 U.S. 200 (1927).

45 C.F.R. Part 46, Protection of Human Subjects.

Estate of C. W., 640 A.2d 427 (Pa. Super. 1994).

Favell, J. E. (1990). Issues in the use of nonaversive and aversive interventions. In S. L. Harris & J. S. Handleman (Eds.), *Aversive and nonaversive interventions*. New York: Springer.

Guardianship of Weedon, 565 N.E.2d 432 (Mass. 1991) (substituted judgment order seeks to give expression to the unique wants and needs of the individual).

Halderman v. Pennhurst State School and Hospital, 446 F. Supp. 1295 (E.D. Pa. 1977) (subsequent history omitted).

Harris, S. L., & Handleman, J. S. (Eds.) (1990). *Aversive and nonaversive interventions*. New York: Springer.

Impact. (1998). Supporting parents who have cognitive limitations (feature issue). *Impact 11(1)*.

In re A. M. S., 419 N.W.2d 723 (Iowa Sup. Ct. 1988).

In re B. S., 693 A.2d 716 (Vt. Sup. Ct. 1997).

In re C. M., 526 N.W.2d 562 (Iowa App. 1994).

In re Caresse B. (Conn. Sup. Ct., March 11, 1997), reported in (1997) *Mental and Physical Disability Law Reporter, 21,* 473.

In re Elizabeth R., 35 Cal. App. 4th 1774 (1995).

In re Hop, 623 P.2d 282 (Cal. 1981).

In re Lindsey C., 473 S.E.2d 110 (W.Va. Sup. Ct. App. 1995).

In re Torrance P., 522 N.W.2d 243 (Wisc. Ct. App. 1994).

In re Welfare of A. J. R., 896 P.2d 1298 (Wash. Ct. App.), *cert. denied,* 904 P.2d 1157 (Wash. 1995).

Lake v. Arnold, 112 F. 3d 682 (3d Cir. 1997).

Lo, B. (1995). *Resolving ethical dilemmas.* Baltimore: Williams and Wilkins.

National Bioethics Advisory Commission (1998). Draft report: *Research involving subjects with mental disorders that may affect decisionmaking capacity.* Available: hhttp://bioethics.gov/bioethics/briefings/jul98/pmdad.pdf

New Mexico v. Penny J., 890 P.2d 389 (N.M. Ct. App.), *cert. denied,* 888 P.2d 466 (N.M. 1994).

N.Y. Stat., Public Health Law Article 24-A § 2440.

NYSARC v. Carey, 393 F. Supp. 715 (E.D. N.Y. 1975), consent decree reproduced in (1976) *Mental Disability Law Reporter, 1,* 65.

Office of the Maryland Attorney General (1998). *Final report of the attorney general's research working group.* Baltimore, MD: Author.

Parham v. J. R., 442 U.S. 584 (1979).

Rehabilitation Act of 1973, 29 U.S.C. § 794 (1998).

Stanley v. Illinois, 405 U.S. 645 (1972).

Stone v. Daviess County Division of children and Family Services, 656 N.E.2d 824 (Ind. Ct. App. 1995).

Symposium: Conducting research on the decisionally impaired (1998). *Journal of Health Care Law & Policy, 1,* 1–300.

T. D. v. New York State Office of Mental Health, 650 N.Y.S. 2d 173 (1996).

Trent, J. W., Jr. (1994). *Inventing the feeble mind: A history of mental retardation in the United States.* Berkeley, CA: University of California Press.

Turnbull, H. R. III. (Ed.). (1977). *Consent handbook.* Washington, DC: American Association on Mental Deficiency.

42 U.S.C. §§ 1983 (1998) and 1985(3) (1998).

Warren, J. W., Sobal J., & Denney, J. H. et al. (1986). Informed consent by proxy: An issue in research with elderly patients. *New England Journal of Medicine, 315,* 1125–1128.

Watkins, C. (1995). Beyond status: The Americans With Disabilities Act and the parental rights of people labeled developmentally disabled or mentally retarded. *California Law Review, 83,* 1415.

Wentzel v. Montgomery County General Hospital, 447 A.2d 314 (Md. 1982), *cert. denied* 459 U.S. 1147 (1983).

Winick, B. J. (1994). How to handle voluntary hospitalization after Zinermon v. Burch. *Administration and Policy in Mental Health, 21,* 395.

Wirsig v. Michigan Protection and Advocacy Services, 573 N.W.2d 51 (Mich. Sup. Ct. 1998).

Wyatt v. Aderholt, 386 F. Supp. 1383 (M.D. Ala. 1974).

Wyatt v. Stickney, 344 F. Supp. 387 (M.D. Ala. 1972) (further history omitted).

Zinermon v. Burch, 494 U.S. 113 (1990).

Zumpano-Canto, J. (1996). Nonconsensual sterilization of the mentally disabled in North Carolina: An ethics critique of the statutory standard and its judicial interpretation. *Journal of Contemporary Health Law and Policy, 13,* 79.

CHAPTER 9

Conclusion

∎

Stanley S. Herr and Joan L. O'Sullivan
University of Maryland School of Law

I n recent years, those working in the field of mental retardation have made great progress in learning to maximize each
person's potential.

They have learned that it is not necessary to make all decisions for those with mental retardation and other developmental
disabilities, but that most such people have the capacity to
express their values and desires and are able to make decisions
for themselves. They recognize that presenting choices and
seeking consent can strengthen a person's sense of autonomy
and self-confidence. Seeking consent to services, housing options, health care, and activities others take for granted enhances
the freedom each person enjoys. In this sense, consent reduces
and eliminates coercion in their lives.

But as options for persons with disabilities increase, so do
areas of conflict. Families, staff, and professionals worry whether
a person's consent is truly informed and voluntary. The impulse
to protect the person from harmful or dangerous choices is
strong. The tension between enhancing autonomy and protecting
the person from harm ebbs and flows, and we realize the need
for more and better communication, more patient explanations,
and more time to understand the wishes of the person. Some
options are so complex that even highly educated individuals
have difficulty deciding what to do. The challenge of explaining
such choices to one with mental retardation can seem overwhelming, and it may be necessary to turn to family, support
networks, and other advisers to reach decisions.

Conclusion

The moral complexity of certain choices compounds the problem. For example, parenting children is an enormous task for any parent. For parents with mental retardation, where the welfare of a third party is involved, allowing total freedom of choice is a risk. But neither should all choices and responsibility be removed from the parent, without regard for the parent's strengths and weaknesses.

Other areas demand understanding and thorough investigation, such as determining whether a person has the capacity to consent to sexual relations. In this area, as in others, we must find the proper balance between autonomy and protection.

Those working in the field must educate themselves about the law and custom of consent in their own states and localities. This educational effort may mean specialized training in consent, considering what constitutes consent, and when it is valid and when not. Professionals should consult with lawyers, psychologists, and other experts in the field to learn the distinctive features of consent in their state. They must learn to determine on an individual basis whether a person is able to consent, and whether that consent is informed. Although this *Guide to Consent* encourages choice, choice should not be offered in a meaningless way, as when, for example, a person's signature is sought on a treatment plan even though the person was not involved in its development. Signing a plan may represent an empowering gesture or recognition of the person's presence but may not reflect actual participation or true understanding. If the consequences of an unwise consent would create difficulty or harm for the person or others, it is better to seek assistance or a surrogate decision.

This *Guide to Consent* presents principles that pose a challenge to those working in the field, families, and self-advocates. We must learn to distinguish when a person has the ability to consent, which choices the person can make, and which the person cannot. When the stakes are high, scrutiny of the choice must be high also.